KT-458-619

The Write Crowd

Literary Citizenship and the Writing Life

Lori A. May

Bloomsbury Academic
An imprint of Bloomsbury Publishing Inc

B L O O M S B U R Y
NEW YORK • LONDON • NEW DELHI • SYDNEY

Bloomsbury Academic

An imprint of Bloomsbury Publishing Inc

1385 Broadway
New York
NY 10018
USA

50 Bedford Square
London
WC1B 3DP
UK

www.bloomsbury.com

**BLOOMSBURY and the Diana logo are trademarks of
Bloomsbury Publishing Plc**

Library of Congress Cataloging-in-Publication Data

The write crowd: literary citizenship and the writing life/Lori A. May.
pages cm
Includes index.
Summary: "Practical tips and examples of how writers of all genres and experience
levels may contribute to the greater literary community"– Provided by publisher.
ISBN 978-1-62892-308-7 (hardback) – ISBN 978-1-62892-309-4 (paperback)
1. Authorship–Social aspects. 2. Creative writing. 3. Mentoring of authors. I. Title.
PN151.M35 2014
808.02–dc23
2014025365

ISBN: HB: 978-1-6289-2308-7
PB: 978-1-6289-2309-4
ePub: 978-1-6289-2310-0
ePDF: 978-1-6289-2311-7

Typeset by Deanta Global Publishing Services, Chennai, India
Printed and bound in the United States of America

The Write Crowd

Contents

Preface vii

1 What is Literary Citizenship? An Introduction 1

2 The Writer and the Writing Life 11

3 Immersion 101: Finding and Creating
Opportunities 23

4 Community (re)Defined 35

5 From the Editor's Desk 53

6 Book Reviewing: Write (about) What you Read 67

7 In Print and Online: Working with Presses and
Journals 83

8 Community Outreach 107

9 In and Outside of Academia 129

10 The Write Direction: Customizing your
Community 145

Appendix A: Community Organizations 161
Appendix B: Sample Book Reviews 169
Acknowledgments 187
Index 189

Preface

Several months prior to making a permanent move from a quaint college town in southwestern Ontario, Canada, to the historic, but rough-edged city of Detroit, I began a research project. There was no real science involved. My intent was to research the community I was about to become a part of and uncover the literary networks already established. I wanted to understand where and when literary activities were taking place. I needed to know what opportunities awaited me—and what opportunities I could create for others.

Just ten days after my international move, with boxes still overflowing and no real geographic sense of direction yet in place, I walked into a poetry reading series knowing not a single person in attendance. I took a seat in the third row—eager, but still nervous about my newness to the area—and before the night's events began, a man approached, introduced himself, and asked who I was.

It's easy to feel intimidated when it's obvious a community is already established—and we're on the outside. It can be uncomfortable, at times, to meet new people and put ourselves out there. Yet, when I reviewed the incredible amount of artistic activity taking place in my new hometown, I knew I had to jump right in. I saw how I could attend a reading in Metro Detroit just about any night of the week. I noticed there were small presses, literary journals, radio programs, and more already working well enough without me. So if I were to immerse myself in this community, if I were to truly feel at home as a writer in this new-to-me city, it was up to me to take the first step.

"I'm a writer," I said. "I'm new in town and this seemed like a good place to meet people." The stranger smiled and nodded. He agreed. He asked a few casual questions to make me feel welcome. Then, he insisted I meet his wife and a few of their friends.

Before the night's reading had even started, I shook hands with this man's wife—who happened to be the organizer of the monthly reading series and the publisher of a small, but well-respected and established literary press. I shook hands with editors, writers of all genres, and readers who expressed a general interest in supporting the arts. When the official events began and the organizer stepped up to the microphone, she made a point to welcome me, the newcomer. She took a moment from her well-planned itinerary to make me feel at home and to ensure others would introduce themselves at the end of the night.

Not all literary events are so welcoming. No. To a writer—anywhere, anytime—it can sometimes feel like there is an "in-crowd" that is guarded like a fortress, impossible for others to penetrate. Yet this was not my experience on this particular night. I was welcomed with open arms and open minds.

It may have been that this was a particularly welcoming group. My experience may have been a fluke, deciding to show up on a night that these folks were in particularly good spirits. Or, it may have been that I showed up with something to offer, something that made me seem like a potential contributor to this literary circle.

Months prior to my move, I knew I wanted to make the transition with something significant to share with my new community. I knew the forthcoming release of a new poetry book was not enough to earn their interest in me as an invested community player. Moving to a new city and just assuming I would find a supportive group to help cheer on and support *my* new publication would not fit the bill when no one knew me; no one had a vested interest in my presence or my forthcoming publication. So I worked and planned and, even before making that move, I put the groundwork in place for a community literary project that would fill a need and provide opportunities to others within the region. This was a project I truly believed in and wanted to see come to life, but the move made the timing seem right. It was.

When I told this group of strangers about the online literary journal I was launching, drawing attention to poetry from the cross-border neighbors of Ontario and Michigan, I had an opening. I got their attention. Sure, I was a writer interested in their community, but I was also immediately offering something outside of myself to that community. In preparation for meeting new people at this particular event, I had taken along fliers for the journal with a call for submissions, the Web site address, and the invitation to get involved. I took along business cards to not only help folks remember me, but also remember the opportunity available to them.

When I was so kindly introduced as a new audience member that night, I felt not as a stranger asking to be let in to an existing group; I felt like I was a thoughtful member-in-waiting. I was hoping to give as much as receive from this community. I wanted to become a part of the literary conversation happening in my backyard.

That night after the reading, I shook hands, took down phone numbers, made lunch plans. The publisher and I met for coffee. We talked about goals and what we could accomplish together. We fed off of one another's drive. She offered for her press to partner for the launch of my literary journal. We decided to host a community event to celebrate the journal—and to introduce my newly published poetry book. We also partnered with an active university press in the city so we could celebrate as much local literary culture as possible. This event was not about me, not exclusively about my book. It was a true community event meant to engage the public and draw attention to our region's thriving literary arts network.

And, within a few short months of living in my new city, after having demonstrated my work ethic, community involvement, and genuine interest in contributing to the larger picture, I was invited to become the Managing Editor of the small press.

Our event was held at a nonprofit arts center. Ten local authors read poems either published in the first issue of my journal or from their new book releases stemming from a number of publishers. The authors had books for sale, while the two partnering presses had tables of their specific titles on hand. More than one hundred members of the public attended. There is no way I would have had such a grand turnout for the release of my poetry book, or for the launch of my literary journal, had I done it on my own and without the support and partnership of others. As a newcomer in town, I didn't even know ten people to personally invite, yet with our combined efforts we drew in more than one hundred. For a poetry event in a small corner of a Detroit suburb, that was impressive.

What most impressed me, though, was how easy it seemed to go from being the newcomer in a strange land to a fully immersed member of the community. During the one night of our event, I met an eclectic mix of authors and readers that immediately expanded my local network and connected me for months and years to come, and continues to connect me to this community. But I shouldn't have been surprised. When we offer more to others than what we ask of them in return, good things happen. When we work to benefit the greater good of our literary circles, everyone benefits.

It doesn't have to take much effort to contribute to the big picture, to become a working part of the whole. I believe in the power of community. I believe in the capability we have, as authors, to not only contribute our own individual creative works, but also help foster and develop our communities and develop meaningful relationships with others.

I am not alone in this mindset. In talking with other writers, editors, and invested readers, I have come to discover some powerful ways in which the literary community is working to support itself, sustain its efforts, and create meaningful opportunities for others to enjoy.

As you explore the chapters throughout this book, I hope you, too, will be inspired to think of ways to further interact within your community. My hope is that you will find ideas for not only enhancing the literary world around you, but also—in turn—enhancing and enriching your own literary life. Because when we feel like we're a necessary part of a community, when we feel connected to others and that we're giving something back, we can't help but benefit. Whether that's the general satisfaction and feeling of goodwill or in seeing new opportunities come our way because of our active role in the community around us, it's a win-win situation. In helping others, we help ourselves.

Personally speaking, my involvement in the community has meant more than supplementing my literary network. By being exposed to a wider diversity of peers, I continually enhance my knowledge and practice of craft. I learn from others and carry with me their inspiration and motivation on and off the page. My literary life has become more vibrant. In attending and participating at events, in connecting with others in my local and national arts community, I have developed real bonds and made friends with people I may not have otherwise encountered. Let's face it: after college, there are only so many ways to connect with like-minded peers and add to our social networks. Supporting and encouraging my fellow writers and contributing to their ambitions has not only made me feel involved as a literary citizen, but I have also experienced the side benefit of connecting on the most basic of human levels—and isn't that what art is meant to do? Through arts involvement, it's possible to not only feel a part of our geographic communities, but also, more importantly, experience that other definition of community—a sense of place and belonging among peers.

In exploring the possibilities shared by myself and others in this book, I hope you are inspired and motivated to become a more involved member of your community. You might surprise yourself, too, in what you can give and what you can gain from giving. You might be surprised to learn how little effort it truly takes to become an active literary citizen.

1

What is Literary Citizenship? An Introduction

Historical context

The term "literary citizenship" may seem like a new buzzword, but the concept is anything but. Near the beginning of the twentieth century, novelists Virginia Woolf and E. M. Forster, together with other influential artists and intellectuals, formed the Bloomsbury Group. While rebelling against a rigid Victorian social structure, the group worked together to discuss and promote its individual and collective artistic goals. The group was "determined to reinvent society,"[1] yet it routinely opened its

---

[1] *Great World Writers: Twentieth Century, Volume 1*, ed. Patrick M. O'Neil (Marshall Cavendish, 2004), 1683.

doors to others in the community by hosting weekly gatherings where writing, art, and societal matters were discussed.

While history has numerous examples of literary citizenship at work, perhaps most often contemporary authors refer back to Walt Whitman's efforts in advocating for a society connected through literature. In the book *Walt Whitman and The World*, contributing author Maria Clara Bonetti Paro credits Whitman not just for his poetic esthetic and defiance against his peers, but also for his stance as a "poet of the present and the singer of the common people and the modern world."[2] Studies of Whitman reveal him as the "people's poet" and we learn of the author's efforts to engage the average working-class person through poetry. Yet, Whitman's goal included more than merely exposing readers to verse. Paro argues that Whitman's vision included a "cosmic consciousness [that] could transform everybody into comrades and equals."[3] In essence, it was Whitman's goal to unite people—writers, readers, *and* the average citizen—through the celebration of literature.

Whitman was not alone in his quest to build community. In a graduate seminar I led at Eastern Michigan University back in 2010, I focused on the work of Whitman and Emerson, and how these nineteenth-century authors provide examples for today's literary citizens. Many of Emerson's lectures focus on self-improvement and on the association between individual and community. In considering identity, Emerson sought to relate

---

[2]Maria Clara Bonetti Paro, "Whitman in Brazil," in *Walt Whitman and The World*, eds. Gay Wilson Allen and Ed Folsom (University of Iowa Press, 1995), 130.
[3]Ibid.

the roles of culture and society. Like Emerson's analysis of the self in society, Whitman voiced in *Leaves of Grass* his concerns of stewardship and equality in a national identity.

It was when Whitman apprenticed with the *Long Island Patriot*—a liberal, working-class newspaper—that he first learned the business of printing and discovered how published words could be immediately communicated to a mass audience.[4] He wrote, edited, and eventually began his own newspaper. For *Leaves of Grass*, Whitman took on the expense of producing the first edition and distributing the book to readers.[5] Yes, one of our most lauded poets in history was a productive self-publisher. But he was also strategic in getting his work noticed. Whitman sent out copies to accomplished writers and when Emerson wrote back with the words, "I greet you at the beginning of a great career," Whitman elected to use this comment—unbeknownst to Emerson—as one of the first promotional blurbs in publishing history.[6]

In the poem, "Poets to Come," from *Leaves of Grass*, Whitman urges the passing on of a legacy, the necessity to perpetually move our society forward:

Poets to come! orators, singers, musicians to come!
Not to-day is to justify me and answer what I am for,

---

[4]Justin Kaplan, *Walt Whitman: A Life* (New York: Harper Perennial Modern Classics, 2003), 74.

[5]Ed Folsom and Kenneth M. Price, "Walt Whitman," *The Walt Whitman Archive*, University of Iowa, Obermann Center for Advanced Studies, 2004. http://www.whitmanarchive.org/biography/walt_whitman/index.html.

[6]Ibid.

> But you, a new brood, native, athletic, continental, greater
>   than before known,
>
> Arouse! Arouse—for you must justify me—you must answer.
>
> I myself but write one or two indicative words for the
>   future,
> I but advance a moment, only to wheel and hurry back in
>   the darkness.
>
> I am a man who, sauntering along without fully stopping,
>   turns a casual look upon you, and
> then averts his face,
> Leaving it to you to prove and define it,
> Expecting the main things from you.[7]

In this poem, Whitman urges others to take responsibility for their art and their role in society. He recognizes that his writing and role in contributing to the literary community is limited and that he will, *or should*, be surpassed by others. Whitman acknowledges that the community must keep moving forward if it is to continue to thrive and grow and engage others.

Contemporary application

In draft mode, writers and other artists may not immediately acknowledge an inevitable audience, yet once a creative work

---

[7] Walt Whitman, "Poets to Come," from *Leaves of Grass*, Bartleby.com, 1999. http://www.bartleby.com/142/90.html.

is complete—that is, ready to share with others—our creations become the catalyst for connecting with others.

"As a writer who has always had one foot on the stage and one on the page, my work is incomplete without human presence," says Laura E. J. Moran, slam poet and cofounder of B-Trads: Teaching Artist Alliance. Moran argues that skilled contemporary artists interact with audiences with the same intent of our artistic predecessors.

> "From the very beginning of what we call humanity when we began making what we call art, taking the images out of our heads and using lines to put them somewhere else outside of us—call it music, call it cave art like that in Lascaux or Chauvet over 30,000 years ago—we have had the need to share stories. Share is the operative word here. No sharing happens without other humans in the room with whom to share. The work then becomes the space between us—not you, not me, not the writing, not the song, but the connection."

Moran points to the historic role of performance in our culture and civilization as a model for audience interaction. "Dare I say, for those writers who must tour or must present even just once . . . understanding basic stage presence and how to respect your audience grants access into a long and beautiful tradition of public engagement beyond commodification. See what Ralph Waldo Emerson had to say on poets and public speaking. He believed it was our duty, *duty*, to engage the public. It is our role and not just an adjunct opportunity to sell product."

Indeed, the contemporary concept of literary citizenship is not unlike Whitman's or Emerson's. Today's writers are actively engaging with their peers and audiences to have an effect on the big picture. They want to have both an immediate impact on their communities and an influence on the future.

So, then, what exactly does it mean to be a literary citizen? Author Kate Gale, the publisher of Red Hen Press, says this: "It means you are not only working on your own creative intellectual work, you are also doing something for the whole literary world. That may be running a reading series, teaching in a Writing in the Schools program, starting a press, or any number of different things."

Literary citizenship takes the power of the individual and puts it to use in fostering, sustaining, and engaging with the literary community for the benefit of others. The concept is to pay kindness and skill forward, to offer something to the community so that others may learn, engage, and grow from combined efforts. And the possibilities for how that is accomplished are wide and varied, both in effort and in outcome. At the heart of literary citizenship, though, is one constant: contributing something to the literary world outside of one's own immediate needs.

In keeping with Whitman's legacy, one critical note is that literary citizenship is not exclusive to some "in-crowd" of well-published writers. Any person, in any town, with any experience—or none whatsoever—in publishing can engage oneself as a literary citizen. Emerging writers and those well established are on equal ground here. Readers and the general community have as much to give and take from literary citizenship as writers have.

The concept of literary citizenship is to promote artistic interest, advocate literature, and foster a cultural well-being.

Diane Tarantini, a graduate student who lives in West Virginia, has this to say: "To me, literary citizenship means membership in a community of folks who enjoy words. These individuals may be people who read and write. They may also be people who are readers only."

As writers, we need one another. We need readers and reviewers, editors and cheerleaders for the highs and lows that invariably come with writing. While the life of a writer continually buoys with the unpredictable waves of publishing, emerging writers especially need mentorship and guidance to weather those uncertainties.

Dinty W. Moore, a renowned author and writing coach, credits his success to those who encouraged him from day one. "My early days as a writer were marked by the usual mistakes: sending juvenile stories to *The New Yorker*, sending out work before it was fully polished, imagining that 'literary stand-out' was a magical splash of fairy dust rather than an honor that is won through ceaseless work and improvement," he says. "But all along the way folks took the time to show me a bit of the path, teach me a small lesson, correct my course in small ways, just as a tennis coach might correct someone's backhand. My success, such as it is, is partly hard work and dedication, but also an accumulation of one thousand moments of generosity from other writers and editors, and the more of us in the literary world who recognize this, who act accordingly, the better the writing world is for everyone."

In fostering our fellow writers, in giving back to our communities and in enhancing what exists and working to develop something new, we not only "pay it forward"[8] by generating goodwill among our peers and community members, but also add to the legacy of our literary circles.

This book will share ways other writers have worked to make things happen. Whether it is in starting independent presses, running a blog to showcase new authors and books, or in volunteering at an already established organization, there are countless ways to get involved. And that's precisely what it comes down to: how we, as writers and readers, can become truly involved, sincerely immersed within the community.

Yet, not all activities that benefit the greater good are the result of volunteering. Later you'll hear from some writers who are making a living after having cultivated an area of need and developing their efforts into money-making businesses. Volunteering one's time is certainly the standard for offering something to the greater community, but a sampling of authors will demonstrate how following one's passion can have unexpected outcomes.

Too, while the ambition of literary citizenship is to help others, to elevate the success of our literary peers, it should not be overlooked that there are most definitely personal rewards. First and foremost is the satisfaction of contributing something for the benefit of others. But, there are also benefits to becoming involved in one's community: we meet peers, editors, reviewers,

---

[8]Catherine Ryan Hyde, *Pay it forward* (Black Swan, 2007).

and others who may, in turn, have something to offer us and may open doors to new opportunities we may not have otherwise discovered while penning alone in the middle of the night with just the sound of our solo breath to guide us.

Even so, one should not consider literary citizenship as a means to an end for personal gain. It is only through authentic engagement, in wanting to give in a heartfelt manner, that we blossom as individuals. Coming into a community only to craftily weave our way through giving, with the sole intent of receiving, is not a masquerade most others will fall for. Such an agenda would also most likely leave you feeling empty if you don't feel that you have been properly "repaid" for your efforts. While it cannot be ignored that the individual benefits from the efforts of the whole, that's not what literary citizenship is about.

Naturally, with good intentions and the desire to contribute to the community, a writer can feel the weight of burden if one overextends oneself. This is sometimes a natural occurrence for any good deed. It can be a challenge to manage one's efforts and the time it takes to engage within the community, help others, and still feel connected to one's own creative energies. Later, you'll see a few real-life examples from authors and editors who have navigated the balancing act between community and personal creative needs, and how they have avoided—or recovered from—burnout.

Whether you consider writing to be a hobby or profession, there is one constant: writers need the support of others. Even nonpublishing writers need the camaraderie that comes from like-minded peers or from family members who understand the lure of the muse and why it is we stay up past a reasonable bedtime.

I hope this book, in sharing the vast experiences of others, will serve as a call to action and inspire you to explore the many ways you may more easily engage with your communities and help contribute to a thriving literary culture. Writing may be a solitary act, but there is no greater thrill than feeling like our words, thoughts, and efforts matter outside of our own selves.

2

The Writer and the Writing Life

Writers write. Some would argue this is all we need to do, perhaps all we should do. After all, writing can take enough of our time and energy—while competing with family life, the day job, and other adult responsibilities—that it may seem difficult enough to protect an hour or two of creative time, let alone to share that time with others. Yet in participating in the broader community, in engaging with others, and sharing our skills and passion with peers and emerging fellows, there is so much joy to experience outside of our individual worlds. We become more.

As a young writer in the making, you no doubt sought out how to become a part of the creative world. You perhaps asked yourself, despite hours spent with a notebook in hand, "Am *I* a writer?" Maybe what you really wanted to know was this: "Do other people see me as a writer?" All it takes to be a writer is an imagination and a pen (or computer). But to feel like a writer, beyond our own words, more often means we desire some sort of acknowledgment from the outside world, be that from readers or peers.

West Virginia writer Diane Tarantini recognizes this need for external acknowledgment and support. "Community engagement provided me the necessary support to a) call myself a writer and then b) to pursue the craft to the best of my ability." It's not merely in calling one's self a writer that we feel a part of this creative world; it's in becoming immersed with the craft—on multiple levels—that we feel a valued part of a working whole.

Being an active member of the community offers rewards big and small. Most common is the feeling of camaraderie and the sense that we are learning more about the fields of writing and publishing. We learn from example. We learn from others. And, sometimes in witnessing another's writing life, we are better able to determine what we ourselves want to accomplish with our craft as we more clearly understand the opportunities available to us.

Tarantini says she often seeks connections with writers who are more established, and perhaps more educated than she is, so that she may learn from them as unofficial mentors. With that motto in mind, Tarranti introduces herself to more experienced writers at community readings and workshops with the intention of making herself available to absorb wisdom. "The quality they bring to an event is tangible to me," she says. "I want to be a Michelangelo of writing, someone who is always still learning."

Writers of all ages and experience levels need the support of others to keep writing, to keep putting ideas on paper. Such support comes from various places: friends, colleagues, peers. Most early support and development comes from education, whether in grade school or in college. And while those in the early stages of artistic development need encouragement, established authors continue to need support in order to weather the doubts, criticism, and weariness that often are a part of the writer's life.

Author and editor Dinty W. Moore says the topic of literary citizenship has always been part of the mission of *Brevity* and the *Brevity* blog as it's an important component of a writer's life—and because he wants to pay forward the encouragement he received throughout his developing career. "My own journey from unpublished writer to a fellow with a few books, some name recognition, essays and stories in a range of magazines, was made possible by the generosity of others—editors who took a chance on my early work, who worked with me to improve my sentences, teachers who mentored me not just on the page but on how a writer lives in the world, other writers who offered encouragement."

Moore says he started the online journal in 1997, "with an eye to giving some of that back, by providing a low rung on the ladder of publication for other new writers to grab hold of. *Brevity* has grown now to where many of our authors are already magnificently-accomplished, but I still have an eye out for the new writer. The blog is an extension of that mission: sharing news, sharing opportunities, helping to define a genre that is still in flux."

As we develop our skills as writers, it should be natural that we want to give some of that support and encouragement back to emerging writers. We all start off as unpublished writers. We all seek the same thing, in one form or another: validation for our work, validation that our voice exists. Encouraging developing writers needn't come by way of formal mentoring exclusively. Any and all of us can effectively lead by example and encourage those around us to keep following their passions.

The writing and publishing community relies on a give-and-take exchange. When we put that much more into enlivening the literary culture around us, when we contribute to the health and vibrancy of our local and found communities, there is more to celebrate and more to pass on to future generations.

Gale Martin, whose novels include *Grace Unexpected*, has been on both ends of this give-and-take spectrum. "I have been the recipient of generous and sometimes unexpected outreach from others. I need to pay that forward. It's the right thing to do in a karma-filled world," she says.

Too, when writing can sometimes feel competitive, when we see others reach success quickly or perhaps with a perceived effortlessness, feeling like a valued part of the community can combat those feelings of fear, envy, and guilt over such thoughts. "Do I ever envy writers who have achieved greater success than me? Absolutely," Martin says. "Does taking an interest in their work and featuring them on my blog or sharing the news of their success mitigate that envy? Absolutely."

Seeing others achieve their goals should be a cause for celebration, but it's less easy to celebrate when we don't have our own supportive community behind us. The camaraderie that comes with feeling actively engaged with others helps with the inevitable highs and lows of writing. Martin says, "It can steel you against the peaks and valleys of the profession—rejection, oversight, negative reviews, and the isolation writers often feel." When we're interested in being a part of a community, in sharing our work and our efforts with others, those peaks and valleys are easier to navigate with the support of like-minded peers.

Roxane Gay, coeditor of *PANK* and a blogger for *HTML-GIANT*, recognizes how the role of the professional writer encompasses more than simply putting one's work out into the world. "Literary citizens acknowledge that being a writer means more than just writing and working in isolation," she says. "We're part of a broader ecosystem and it's important to engage with that ecosystem by reading the work of others, supporting literary magazines and organizations, mentoring younger writers, and finding ways to advocate for the importance and enduring power of the written word." In contributing to a broader network, Gay has discovered the benefits of being involved. "Community involvement has always helped me grow as a writer and person. It makes me feel less alone."

When we embrace the community, we gain a better understanding of the creative world in which we participate. We feed off one another's successes and boost one another up when rejections come in. Yet, literary citizenship is not merely about engaging with other writers. Yes, there are writers and readers to connect with, but a broader society—as Whitman recognized—can also benefit from literary outreach. After all, don't we all want to see more readers in the world?

Michigan writer Loreen Niewenhuis, author of *A 1000-Mile Walk on the Beach* and *A 1000-Mile Great Lakes Walk*, looked at ways to reach a vast audience and engage new readers. One out-of-the-box way she accomplished this was in approaching stores that don't usually sell books. "Since my book has a nature/environmental message," she says, "I've been able to get it into several nature stores and at least one store that had an environmental awareness angle—hemp clothing, mittens made from recycled sweaters, all-natural cleaning products."

While this may be a great marketing approach, Niewenhuis was most keen on capturing an attentive audience that may not have otherwise discovered her writing. In doing so, she has gained the interest of a few nonreaders and helped them discover literature in a new and unexpected way. "The owner featured my book on a table just as you walked into the store. I brought along rocks and shells and made a little display about Lake Michigan to really make it special." She made her work accessible to a broader public and took the time to find ways to bring literature into a nontraditional reading environment.

Niewenhuis never forgets, though, the value of the bookseller and she is adamant in ensuring the local independents are active in her book release plans. "I believe in the importance of the independent bookstore to our communities and to literature as a whole. When my first book was getting close to being released, I asked my publisher if we could just sell it to the indies. I believe he chuckled at this notion at the time because once a book is put into distribution, it's available to all vendors. I personally visited indie bookstores on my hiking route and introduced myself to managers and owners."

In reaching out to smaller shop owners, Niewenhuis aimed to develop relationships with others who would enjoy her work and feel the benefits of seeing an author visit their community. The author had over 70 events related to the release of her first book and many of these took place in small towns and lakeshore villages—areas that are not often visited by touring authors.

"Communities off the beaten literary path appreciate it when authors make an appearance in their communities," says Niewenhuis. "Since most of my events like this took place near Lake Michigan, people living there had a connection to that body of water and I could connect with them by discussing the lake. *Any* event a writer has should be treated as a time to make connections with people. That's the focus, not selling books."

Establishing relationships with independent booksellers aid both the artistic and business elements of the writing life. Like any other vocation, writers need to understand the inner workings of the writing and publishing world. Having a close relationship with local booksellers helps us understand how sales and marketing works, how events are planned, and how readers connect with our works. In understanding this part of the process, it's like getting a free education in publishing straight from those who know it best.

While there are skills to be learned in working with booksellers, Niewenhuis emphasizes that there is more to partnering with local booksellers than simply asking them to stock your book and host your events. It's about establishing relationships and giving back more than what one expects to take. Niewenhuis says it's important to "browse. Pick something to buy. Buy it." The local shops need our support as much as we need theirs and being an active part of that cycle will ensure that the bookseller sees you as a serious partner in reaching readers and, as Niewenhuis says, "not just another kook who comes in to try to sell them a book."

There may at times feel like there is a fine line between being an active literary citizen and being someone who uses every opportunity to market his work. The reality of publishing today is that we writers are most often required to sell and market our books and draw in new readers one way or the other. Being an active literary citizen, though, requires our involvement apart from the business side of writing. Paying visits to bookstores—when we need nothing from them other than a friendly hello—and attending other writers' readings—because we want to support *their* work—all piece together to make us involved members of the community seeking engagement, and not just reward.

In this way, it may be easiest to consider that writers have three roles to fulfill: the creative process of generating stories, the publicity and marketing aspects publishers come to expect from us, and the community engagement that comes along with being an active literary citizen. The writing always comes first, hands down. The other two components are optional for some writers, but marketing is more and more an expected part of accepting a book deal. Publishers want to see us out there and generating interest in our work through readings, lectures, book signings, and all of the other tasks that can sometimes feel like robbing the creative time. Yet, it's a necessary part of the business, at least on some level, at least for most of us.

Literary citizenship, though, is optional. It's not necessary for an author to give time to the community. It's not mandatory to encourage fellow writers or to encourage an emerging voice. None of this is necessary to writing and publishing, nor should it be seen as a means to an end. No one should expect to earn a book contract because of contacts made in their literary circles. No one should think that being nice to a few folks will make them a bestseller. And, yet, giving something back to the literary community and to the community at large still *feels* good. You can't help but feel more valued as a writer when others are excited about your presence. We are drawn to those who are not just successful, but also sincerely engaged with, and care about, others. It's not always about charisma, either, but about being authentically concerned with being present, with seeing others succeed just for the sake of cheering them on. Success, too, is not just about publishing. Witnessing the artistic growth and development of our peers is its own reward. That's success; that's gratifying on its own level and sometimes more rewarding than seeing a publication credit.

While literary citizenship is not a mandatory component to one's writing life, many authors feel it intrinsic for their own sense of place, their sense of well-being. Others find that it is nearly impossible to conduct writing business without the support of others and the only way to earn that support is in being involved—well before you need something from your community.

Being present is what it's truly about. While much of this book aims to demonstrate how to create and share opportunities with others, being an active literary citizen does not require starting something from scratch. After all, supporting what already exists around us is the first and most basic step in helping our communities thrive. Visiting authors hope to see a welcoming audience at their readings and talks. The simple act of showing up and being present is what matters.

"There is a chemistry to a room you cannot replicate anywhere else. A good crowd in the right room is transformative—not only for the audience but for the writer as well," says Jim Warner, columnist for *Sundog Lit* and Managing Editor of *Quiddity*. "You spend countless nights behind a desk, at a kitchen table, talking to no one, and trying to connect. The best art is conversation and the best reading works the same way. An audience closes the circuit. You make eye contact. You feel them follow you. If you're mindful of the crowd, they help shape your reading—the energy, the catharsis, the shared joy. . . . You are mainlined into community and connection."

It can sometimes feel intimidating to walk into a public reading and take a seat among strangers. It's important to recognize that most presenting authors also have nerves—that no one will show up, that their work may be misunderstood, that they may miss a line in a poem they've worked hard to refine on the page. Your presence reassures the guest reader that the work matters, that their writing is appreciated.

Too, some people talk themselves out of attending an event as they have no intention of buying books on site. Rest assured, a visiting author is more interested in seeing an audience show up and enjoying the connection through literature not replicated elsewhere. "Whether they buy a book or not doesn't matter," Warner says. "Whether there are three or three hundred in attendance doesn't matter. I think about seeing readings at St. Mark's Place or hearing someone like Patricia Smith and it's the moment of interconnectivity I felt which still remains. The chance to be a part of that type of connection makes the world just a little smaller and maybe the seat time at the desk or kitchen table or dingy diner on a Tuesday night seem that less lonely."

Supporting the literary community needn't cost money. Helping emerging writers develop their voice, supporting what others are doing, and cheering on the successes of peers needn't be time consuming either—and shouldn't be seen as burdensome tasks. A little effort and time can indeed go a long way.

These discussions of literary citizenship should be considered as buffet options, wherein a writer may pick and choose what works for him or her. Later in this book, we'll hear from several writers who will share ways to balance creative and community efforts while avoiding burnout. Writing must always come first, so in the next chapter we'll look at numerous ways to connect with others—with a variety of commitment and personal comfort levels—that may inspire you to customize your own involvement as a literary citizen.

3

Immersion 101: Finding and Creating Opportunities

The concept of literary citizenship has been echoed and popularized across the country and beyond, and in various ways: cultural citizenship, arts or cultural ambassadorship, and the like. Whatever you call it, the concept is the same. It's about getting involved beyond one's own writing to contribute to the bigger picture. Writers such as Kate Gale, Dinty W. Moore, Jane Friedman, David W. Fenza, Caroline See, and Cathy Day are some of the folks you may have heard use the term or speak about the concept of literary citizenship. There are countless others. Frankly, the more people who discuss ways to engage in and promote literature the better.

Yet when considering how to become an active literary citizen, it's important to distinguish what one should expect—and not expect—as a result of contributing your time, energy, and personal funds invested to the community.

What to expect from literary citizenship

Contributing your time to the community might make you feel good. It should. But, there is a fine line between finding a sustainable balance and cornering one's self as a result of overextending. There is such a thing as giving too much, particularly if it robs you of your own writing time. Writing must always come first. When that need is well protected, though, offering your time and skills to the outside world can create a sense of purpose, well-being, and goodwill. You might feel like you are a more integral member of your community when you volunteer a few hours a week or month. You may feel like you're becoming an influential part of the equation. It's possible you'll see the results of your efforts—but you might not. Thus, *expecting anything* from literary citizenship may jeopardize what should feel good. It's like any volunteer or charitable work; the benefit is in the act of giving, and any positive outcome should be considered a bonus.

What not to expect

Fame. Fortune. Constant thanks and praise for doing something good. Instant connections and a get-published-quick pass. Literary citizenship shouldn't be considered a down payment for future rewards. Yes, most often what we put into the literary community comes back to us in some regard, but anticipating a turn on the receiving end may leave a writer feeling bittersweet and empty-handed.

Instead, consider what you can realistically offer and what time you can conceivably give without sacrificing your writing time. The answer will be different for everyone and may change over time. This is particularly the case when assessing an idea with a long-term vision. Starting a literary journal or a nonprofit organization not only requires foresight when planning time and funds, but also requires the involvement of other people who will come to depend on you for leadership; on the flipside, you may not find the necessary assistance from others and be left to manage a large project on your own.

These are all things to assess as you consider your comfort level in community engagement. Like Loreen Niewenhuis, you may find it best to dedicate a specific time of year to your own work and not allow other events and community activities to interfere with your reserved writing time. Or, you may find it easier to contribute in bits and pieces, through social media or local events, rather than committing to a bigger, more long-term project.

Determining personal strengths and personal commitment levels

There are countless ways by which we may contribute to the literary community. Here, though, is a basic list of some of the things anyone, anywhere can become more involved in. Consider your own skills and time availability when reviewing this list and use it as a prompt to come up with any number of other opportunities tailored to your own interests.

The basics

Write. Be passionate about and protective of your writing time. By putting your writing first, you'll demonstrate your enthusiasm and love of the art. This, on its own, may be enough to encourage another person to follow one's dreams and write that memoir one's been thinking about. Passion is contagious.

Read. Tell others about the books you love. There's no need to spend much money. Go to the library or shop at used bookstores. Support the indie bookstores in your community when you can. Keep your eye out for sales. Create a book swap with friends to help one another discover new titles.

My father, a nonwriter, keeps a stash of books in his vehicle to give to others. When he spots a book that would appeal to someone he knows, at a yard sale or flea market, he adds the book to his library-on-wheels. He'll pick up titles that seem interesting or rare, even if he doesn't immediately know anyone to give it to, knowing he'll find a reader for it in time. My father loves to read—and loves to see others reading.

Spread the word. Read literary journals and share what you love with others. Give your copy to someone else when you're done. Tell a friend about a submission call. Donate used copies of journals to your library or after-school program. Keep them on hand when you have writing events or workshops to leave out for others to take.

Help others read. Think of those with less access to books like low-income communities or remote rural areas without libraries. Offer an author talk, reading club, or a writing workshop to youths or the elderly in a community center. Donate books and writing supplies for programs already in existence.

Gather community members to help start a program to teach literacy or grammar skills. If you're able to do so, contribute time or money to a national organization already in place like Girls Write Now, the PEN Prison Writing Program, or a regional branch of 826 National that offers "programs that provide under-resourced students, ages 6–18, with opportunities to explore their creativity and improve their writing skills."[1] Leave a used book behind at the dental office, auto repair shop, or local skating rink. Leave a book on the train, plane, or other transit. Connect with others on BookCrossing.com.

Encourage other writers. Take an interest in others' writing lives. Offer support and attend their readings and events. Share your own ups and downs with a fellow author who is experiencing discouragement. Take a fledgling writer out for coffee or send an email welcoming the writer to talk out his or her writing concerns.

---

[1] 826 National: http://826national.org.

Share opportunities. One of the perks of being involved in the lit community at large is coming across opportunities—for internships, jobs, grants and fellowships for arts colonies or retreats, and more. Yet, there are only so many of these you can take advantage of personally. One of my favorite hobbies is sharing such discoveries with my peers. When I see a call for submissions for the kind of work a peer writes, I ensure he or she knows about it; when I see an exciting job or fellowship opportunity that seems perfect for another peer, I share the news with him or her. If you see an incredible opportunity that isn't quite right for you for whatever reason, think of somebody you know who may consider it a perfect fit and pass it on.

Write thank you notes. Extend the conversation and build relationships with peers. Thank hosts of literary events in your community for doing what they do. Send a note to a literary journal to let it know how much you've enjoyed its latest issue. Carolyn See, author of *Making A Literary Life*, suggests that writers take the time to send "charming notes" to others, to show appreciation for a good book, to send thanks to an editor who took the time to offer feedback, and to help encourage peers.[2]

Write to authors whose books you enjoy, not expecting a note in return from Margaret Atwood or Stephen King, but because it will make you feel good and make them feel good. Don't sell

---

[2]Carolyn See, *Making A Literary Life* (Random House, 2002), 37.

yourself as an author. Just let them know you enjoyed their work. If you can't reach an author, send a note to his or her agent or editor. These folks will most always pass on good news and praise. Plus, it lets publishers know firsthand that readers are enjoying the work of their authors.

With a bit of time

Develop an online presence. Join online communities where you can talk about books and writing. SheWrites, GoodReads, Red Room, and many other such online communities are dedicated to talking about authors and writing. Use your Facebook, Twitter, and other social media accounts to share your reading list and help others spread word about their events.

Interview authors. Use your blog or someone else's to conduct interviews with authors you know or those who have a new book coming out. You may find markets to publish author interviews, but a simple way to provide content on your blog is to share what other writers are doing. Start small by conducting Q&As with writers in your region. Branch out to authors you discover on Facebook or other online communities. Interview writers who are working on their first book and help them draw attention to their short pieces in literary journals. Catch up with your fellow alums and share what they're working on now.

Review books. This may be done formally with print or online magazines, newspapers, and literary journals. Consider the more informal review, too, for online bookstores and general retailers, peers' blogs, in your social media feed, and even in your alma mater's newsletter. Chapter 6 shares more insight into why book reviewing is so important to our culture and includes interviews with others who consider reviewing as a necessary part of their literary lives.

Read the slush pile. Volunteer to be a reader for a literary journal. Not only will you be helping a journal with its workload, but also you'll earn a hands-on education related to publishing. Jennifer McGuiggan, a writer, editor, and writing coach from PA, wrote about her early editorial experience with *Hunger Mountain*:

> When the opportunity to be a submission reader for *Hunger Mountain* came along, I thought it was a great chance to learn about a journal from the inside out. I also hoped that it might bring me some good *juju*, a little cosmic extra credit when it came time for *me* to start submitting to journals. . . . After months of wading through the CNF slush pile, I learned firsthand a truth about the world of journals: they turn down more pieces than they accept. My delusions of grandeur now tempered (I was never that deluded to begin with), I submitted an essay to a journal contest. It was no shock when I received that first rejection. . . . By the time two more rejections arrived, I had created a robust spreadsheet to organize my ever-growing list of journals. The array of possibilities both excited and overwhelmed me, but mostly I was happy to have these three rejections. It meant I was part of the community. The combination of submitting my work and volunteering

at *Hunger Mountain* made me feel like I'd passed part of the citizenship test for the Land of All Things Literary.[3]

Volunteer at events. Help set up chairs at a local reading series. Offer to help publicize a literary festival. Use your design skills to rework an art center's Web site. Help out at the book sales table, fetch refreshments, help market and fundraise, or be the person who picks up an author from the airport. Introduce your professional and business skills to local and regional organizations and ask where the need is greatest.

Mentor others. Emerging writers vary in age. Volunteer to judge a poetry contest at a retirement residence. Give a guest talk for a high school English class. Take someone up when he or she asks if you'll read his work. Go ahead and limit it to a few pages, but extend this generosity at least once in your life. Give the writer critical feedback and direction, and share a few resources where the writer may gain further mentorship.

With a bit of money

Pay writers. When in the position to ask a favor of a writer and you can afford to do so, offer a few bucks to a writer when requesting mentorship or critiques. Writers are asked frequently to "look something over" or "give some feedback." Many will and do this sort of thing for peers, in good will, in good faith. But if

---

[3]Jennifer McGuiggan, *Hunger Mountain,* blog. http://www.hungermtn.org/literary-citizenship.

you can afford more than a thank you note, give more than a thank you note. If that's a few bucks, great. But any other token of appreciation can be equally appreciated: a signed book (from you or another author), a coffee shop or bookstore gift card, a coffee or lunch date when you see each other at a national conference. No matter how, be thankful and gracious to whom you are asking something of, and remember that person's generosity; then pay it forward to another writer someday, when you're in the position of being asked for help.

Subscribe to journals. Support the places you want to print your work. It needn't be expensive. Alternate subscriptions each year to spread the wealth and expose yourself to new voices. Enter journal contests. Most offer a subscription with a contest submission fee, so you have the twofold benefit of submitting and supporting their efforts. Do your research for the most reasonable and favorable opportunities and budget one or two contest subs for the year. Tell peers you are doing so and encourage others to submit. Help journals discover new talent—and generate funds to keep publishing.

Support peers. Buy books from authors you know, even if you're not necessarily interested in the topic. A friend has a book on organic gardening and you prefer fiction? Support that friend anyways; you can always give the book as a gift.

When I visit independent bookshops, I look for the local author section and seek out a book signed by the author. Even if I don't know that author personally, this is a simple way to support both the indie bookseller and a writer local to the area. It also gives me an opportunity to write to that author to say where I picked up his or her book and to tell that author what I enjoyed about that person's writing.

Start a journal or small press. This sort of commitment certainly takes more time, energy, and money to be sustainable, but it's a worthy venture if you have the passion for it. An online journal is much less costly and poses more accessibility by reaching a potential worldwide audience. Whether quarterly or monthly, you'll need the support and efforts of others to help edit, design, and solicit content, not to mention get the word out to readers. In Chapter 7, we'll hear personal experiences from several writers who started literary journals, small presses, and medium-sized indies. Ask questions. Learn from others. Or, help fund a small press or journal that already exists. Give your time and/or money to support those who have taken the risk, and help reap the reward of sustainability.

Start an organization. Perhaps you have an idea for a business or a nonprofit that can help emerging writers or young readers. It may seem like a daunting task, but every organization starts with a simple vision. Talk to others who have made an impact in the greater community. It took more than one person to fully develop She Writes, VIDA, Canadian Women in the Literary Arts, Cave Canem, etc., and all of those groups we value as a part of our culture. Find others who share your passion and talk to the founders of organizations. Ask how they have allotted their time, energy, and financial commitments, as running an organization requires an investment in each of these aspects. Listen to their advice and start drafting your own plans; or, consider what you may offer to an organization already in existence.

Leave a legacy. Talk to your alma mater about establishing an endowment fund to help future emerging writers in need. Speak with your accountant and lawyer about your estate plans. Consider donating a lasting gift to a journal, literary center, awards program, or educational group.

Customizing your literary life

It doesn't matter how much time or money you can offer to the community. What matters most is that you find authentic ways to connect and contribute. Literary citizenship needn't cost any money. It needn't take much time. The ideas listed above are mere ideas. There are countless others not listed and many more yet to be discovered. In seeing what others are doing, in reviewing the various opportunities available to you, it's up to you to determine to what extent you can offer your time, skills, and financial support. Regardless of how much or how modest your involvement is, your community and peers will benefit and, in turn, so will you.

4

Community (re)Defined

Now that we've looked at some of the many ways by which writers can engage with others, you may be considering how to make things happen in your own community. Perhaps you live in a smaller town or a rural area that does not have a cornucopia of events already in place. But there is no such thing as a group too small when it comes to literary citizenship. Starting a monthly, quarterly, or semiannual gathering of writers in a community center or regional library branch may be the catalyst for additional engagement. Online activities, too, can certainly open up your connection to others, be it through a virtual workshop, blog exchange, or a social networking site that bridges geographic gaps. Later in this chapter, we'll hear from writers who have taken that route with positive results.

If you live in a city, perhaps you feel that there is already enough activity taking place. If that's the case, consider contributing your skills and interests to community groups already in existence. There is no need to reinvent the proverbial wheel if there is already an abundant selection of activity in your area. Just because your region has an established calendar of events, though, does not mean there is no room for the support of additional readers and writers.

When I made the move from Ontario to Michigan, I was pleasantly overwhelmed with the amount of readings, workshops, and other literary events taking place in Metro Detroit. While I was excited to contribute time and effort to what already existed, I started a regional online literary journal as a way to offer even more of my investment in the work of others. I was particularly interested in connecting these bordering regions through literature. Yet, it's not necessary to create a new opportunity to show your support of the community; those that organize current events are often in need of help from other locals.

"Good literary citizens find ways to benefit other members of the community. Volunteering with a local writers' group would be one possibility," says Wayne Ude, director of the Whidbey Writers Workshop. He suggests helping with something as simple as "showing up early to help set up the chairs, which can establish your intention to support the community rather than simply expecting it to support you."

Readers and writers alike who have a mere hour or two a month may find helping an established group fits with a busy schedule. That may be setting up a room for a reading, picking up refreshments for an event reception, or helping an author at the book sales table.

Community can be defined more broadly than ever, and it is ours to create, support, and foster. Community is not bound by geographic borders; it is an emotional, intellectual, and artistic sense of place that has unlimited potential for growth and development.

Fostering literary boroughs

There are a number of cities that come to mind when one thinks of a thriving literary center: New York, Los Angeles, Chicago, Toronto, Paris, London, and more. Yet, we don't all have access to a cultural metropolis—and some of us choose to live a much quieter life.

"Though I certainly would welcome the chance to visit NYC again," says Susan Tekulve, author of *In the Garden of Stone*, "I don't think I could live there now because there *is* so much to do, and I'd be out all the time, and I'd be too distracted and exhausted to write."

Personally, this is something I very much relate with, as my few years spent in Toronto were some of my busiest—as far as connecting with others and enjoying all the culture the city had to offer—yet also some of my least productive years for writing. When I later lived in a smaller college town in southwestern Ontario, I was much more focused on my own writing, even while venturing out to the occasional reading or author talk. I needed the time, the space, and the (more) quiet area to balance both endeavors. Feeding off the energy of others is one thing; seeing one's writing time suffer from too many social commitments is another.

This is why Tekulve embraces the comfort of her smaller community. "I've heard it said that the best writing spaces force a person to look inward. So living in a relatively rural, sleepy Southern mill town gives me ample time to look inward," she says. "That said, you'd be surprised by how many different opportunities there are to meet terrific writers where I live."

The author and instructor helps run the visiting writers series at Converse College in Spartanburg SC, where she has taught for close to two decades. The program brings in five writers a year for the undergraduate program and at least ten a year for the Master of Fine Arts residencies. Tekulve says that in connecting with these visiting writers, many become long-distance writing friends that she maintains contact with online and at conferences around the country.

"I guess I've seldom felt overlooked or out of touch with other writers," says Tekulve, "but I watch the news coming out of South Carolina, and, sadly, the nightly news has a way of portraying South Carolina in ways that don't always sound literate, or smart. It occurs to me that maybe people from other regions might perceive that this area of the South is out of touch with all things literary."

Yet with five different colleges in the area and a thriving bookshop in town, Tekulve has found a number of local reasons to celebrate. "The bookstore is a marvel because it is completely non-profit," Tekulve says of Hub City Bookshop. The shop's owner, Betsy Teter, is also the director of a small press. Tekulve adds that Teter "directs community writing workshops and literary events all year long. So while I have access to writers who come in through Converse, I also can attend readings and workshops hosted by Hub City."

When a local college hosts a visiting writer, that writer will often offer a workshop at Hub City. This sort of cross-collaboration encourages contact among local readers and writers, and adds to the regional offerings.

"I don't ever feel a lack of contact with other writers, and certainly I think I live in a community of readers," says Tekulve. "In some ways, a small, out-of-the way Southern town is the perfect place for a writer to live because I'm not surrounded by people who all have the same exact experiences that I have had. Also, Spartanburg really isn't that out of the way, or that rural, and there is a strong arts movement right here in town. We're just an hour south of Asheville, North Carolina, and two hours north of Charleston, South Carolina, and both of these towns are sophisticated literary hubs."

It's sometimes surprising to learn of a vibrant literary culture taking place in a smaller area. Some cities, too, are not always at the forefront when we think of booming literary centers. It was for this reason that *Ploughshares*, a journal based out of Emerson College in Boston, began the "Literary Boroughs" series on their blog.

When it was announced that the annual Association of Writers and Writing Programs (AWP) conference would be hosted in Boston in 2013, the *Ploughshares* team wanted to do something to celebrate their local writing community. "Although Boston is well known as a center of academia, it is not known as the main hub of the literary world the way New York City is," says Andrea Martucci, former managing editor of *Ploughshares*. "Despite that, there is a thriving literary community with a long history. This got us to thinking about how there are tons of other communities around the country and around the world that have a small but highly active literary ecosystem, and we decided that we would dedicate almost a year to highlighting some of them on the blog, leading up to the post about our own literary community."

Martucci announced their plans via social media and the response was immediate and overwhelming. Writers, she says, were thrilled for the opportunity to talk about what they enjoyed in their own local communities and comment on those they've discovered while traveling. Yet, it wasn't just mid-sized cities that were being hailed as thriving cultural centers. Martucci heard from writers residing across the world, as far as Morocco, who wanted to share what was happening in their regions.

The result was that *Ploughshares* was able to share a wealth of information about far-off towns and cities that want to increase awareness of their activities and invite others to visit. The towns of Omaha NE, Columbia MO, Great Falls MT, Laramie WY, and Denton TX may not immediately come to mind when one thinks of a booming literary center, yet these are just a few of the areas *Ploughshares* featured in the series.

"Once the posts were up, it was really great to see the reactions of the local readers and writers who were proud to call their city home," she says. "The posts garnered a lot of attention locally, and many local media sources picked up on the series. Readers familiar with the area left comments on the blog to contribute additional people or places in the city that were notable. It was rewarding to see people collaborating and joining in the conversation in that way. In addition, a lot of people from other places left comments on Facebook or on the blog saying that they were excited to visit the places."

In compiling a series focused on literary boroughs, Martucci says a theme emerged. "Almost all of them had one or more local bookstores or a great library system, almost all had some sort of institute of higher education or a writing center, and almost all of them had local writers, and establishments or parks that were conducive to writing." What wasn't clear, Martucci says, was how these communities developed, as "there's the chicken or egg question—did these elements develop organically and the literary community followed, or was it first necessary for the people who make up that community to be present and thus develop those resources?"

Most likely, it's a little of both. Without an audience—no matter how small—a fledgling event series will crumble. Conversely, without events and opportunities to explore, community members are limited in what they may achieve. So, how does one contribute to building a stronger community in one's own locale?

"I think the first thing you should do is find your people," Martucci says. "This was something that the series demonstrated again and again. You could have a town full of readers and writers, but the key element that makes it a community is the interaction and collaboration. If there's no existing literary community to speak of, start small. You could start a monthly meet-up in a coffee shop, or a book club that meets in the library. Start spreading the word, and I think you'll be surprised by the number and kinds of people who come out of the woodwork. Once you've established a base audience or a gathering place for like-minded people, I think collaboration and further development will start to happen organically."

While that may be so, organic development does not happen or sustain itself without effort. Promoting an event and diversifying the audience by inviting the community at large will turn a narrow-focused activity into a more inviting atmosphere. This concept, Martucci says, applies to both regional and national events. "The bookfair at the annual AWP conference is great because we get to meet writers at every stage of their career, but I also really enjoy events like the Boston Book Festival because we meet so many people who are first and foremost readers," she says. "They are just as excited about literature as the writers, and I think it's extremely important for literary communities to foster and encourage that group of readers because they are the ones who are the patrons of the literary arts."

Not every town has a sizeable population of writers, but it may have a larger population of readers hungry for the opportunity to talk about books. It only takes one invested writer or reader to open the door to connect with others. If your town does not have a bookstore or library within driving distance, consider organizing a book discussion series in the town hall, a church basement, outdoor gathering space, or other publicly accessible location.

Community events needn't be formal. Poet Cecilia Stormcrow Llompart, author of *The Wingless*, took a more personalized approach to introducing her work to others. "I gave a poetry reading in my own living room once," she says. "My mother was visiting and I realized that she had never heard me read to an audience before, so I invited a handful of peers over and made dessert and provided drinks and crowded them around me for a fraction of the evening."

No microphone was required. There were no posters advertising the reading. Yet, Llompart noticed something remarkable happening during this intimate event. She says her living room audience "looked perfectly relaxed, even happy, even enchanted in the dim light. And I said to them, '*this* is why we do it—please don't forget that when you leave this room.' I don't know how many of them understood what I was referring to, though I saw some nods. But there has to be some reason why we, as poets at least, suffer through the pomp and the programs and the poverty—some reason far more pervasive than what happens between the pen and the page. And when I read my poems aloud to people, when I can actually see the place where those poems touch the soul—it isn't in the numbers at all. It's in the faces."

Any fan of literature in any part of the world can host a meaningful event—anywhere. In living rooms and backyards, in the lunchroom at work, the venue is not the important part. It is always the connection to others over the love of literature that matters. "I'd rather give a thousand readings to a party of one, than one reading to a crowd of a thousand, as long as I know someone is listening in a way that actually changes them," says Llompart. "And I like to think other poets feel the same. That the number of seats filled means poetry is well today— look, people are excited, and they came out, not for me, but for poetry."

It's not the quantity of attendees or the frequency of events that matter. What matters is the attempt to connect like-minded members of the community through a shared interest in reading and celebrating the arts. Plus, in starting small with more personalized events, a host may gradually see a larger interest develop over time.

One way to maximize audience potential is to consider what other cultural activities are taking place in your area. Brian Fanelli, author of *Front Man*, co-developed a reading series in the Scranton and Wilkes-Barre area of Pennsylvania. Together with writer Jason Lucarelli, the hosts established the event series at New Visions Studio and Gallery. This has led to some crossover for arts patrons and literary types alike.

"During our last reading, we had acoustic music," Fanelli says. "The gallery usually has art work up for the readings, too, so during the break and before and after the reading, attendees have a chance to view the work of local artists."

Fanelli had previous experience in running reading series' and open mic events in Philadelphia and wanted to see that vibrancy come to life in his new locale. "When I lived in the Philly area, I attended so many different mics. I got my start reading when I was 18 or 19, and it gave me confidence in my work. It also connected me with other writers who were mentors to me and encouraged me to keep writing."

The author says focusing on local writers helps draw attention to the creativity happening around them, but also provides a support system to emerging writers. Since their start, the hosts have featured students from local writing programs and published writers visiting the area, yet their focus has always been on featuring local voices in the early stages of their writing lives. In supporting the locals, the hosts have found a return in support from their communities.

"The New Visions series, and others like it in the area, have proved you don't have to live in a big city to have a strong literary scene. You just need people willing to put in the time and effort to organize the events, and you need a community willing to support it," says Fanelli. "We've had a lot of folks attend the reading series that aren't necessarily writers, and people that have said they never enjoyed poetry until coming to one of the New Visions readings. This has meant a lot to us. We want to show that poetry and prose can be for everyone, not just part of academia and PhD and MFA programs. During each reading, I see a different face in the crowd, and that's meant a lot to me. I want to continually reach out to new people."

Exposing young minds to a variety of genres and opportunities is what Heather Taylor, coordinator of the McCann Writing Center at Bethany College, also had in mind. With a town population hovering around just one thousand, Bethany WV may not seem like a literary hotspot, but Taylor has ensured that her students receive not only academic writing support, but an education in culture as well. She says one of the most successful components of creating a community of young writers "has been the poetry slam. I think students have certain preconceived notions about what it means to be a writer and a poet. The slams have been a great way to reach out to students who would not normally participate."

Taylor creates an open mic venue for student writers and pushes them to explore poetry outside of the academic environment by introducing them to award-winning authors and slam champions like Jason Carney, the Texas-based author of *Starve the Vulture: One Man's Mythology*. "I think it's important for students to be exposed to all different types of writing," Taylor says. "In the days leading up to a slam, I'll show some videos in the Writing Center and a discussion usually follows."

She has also introduced her students to other facets of the writing life. "I had the opportunity to plan and host a book release party for a member of the English faculty," she says. "We hosted a party when Dr. Brandon Dean Lamson's Juniper Prize-winning book of poems was released. The students involved were able to see what goes into planning such an event. We had a local bookstore come in to sell books, as well as the usual of booking the location, getting the food, and setting up the technology." This experience educates emerging writers while involving them in the process of supporting others, and Taylor's efforts demonstrate how even a small town can create meaningful opportunities for engagement.

Creating connections online

Regardless of geographic locale, readers and writers alike can connect with others interested in literature and creative writing. Thanks to the internet, we are no longer tethered to our physical locations. While that means there are opportunities to connect with far-away readers and writers, some authors find that the internet also works as a tool to enhance their local communities.

Nathan Summerlin, a Pennsylvanian writer and designer, began an online resource for the local writing community. 570 Writers, which gives a nod to the local area code, has been active for a few years and helps interested attendees find literary events in the area.

"I wanted to make it a little easier for people to connect and promote local events and news relating to writers," he says. "I think writers are usually happy to see any signs of support. Brian Fanelli, who's also based in the area, volunteered to lend a hand early on, and he's been helping to keep the site updated since."

Summerlin says the response has been very positive from readers and writers alike. And, while he has been surprised at times with how many local events are happening in the region, the task of sharing literary events with others is manageable and a unique way by which he can contribute his Web design skills for the benefit of others. "It's a pretty small investment of time now that it's up and running," Summerlin says.

Yet, one needn't have professional design skills to connect with others via the internet. Blog platforms have become more user-friendly in recent years and authors may use these not only as tools to share their own news, but also as a way to engage readers across the literary spectrum.

Matt Bell, a Michigan-based author whose books include *How They Were Found*, uses his social media accounts and author Web site to connect with other readers. Since 2006, the author has been sharing a personal, cumulative reading log of the hundreds of books he's enjoyed. "I grew up in an area where there wasn't much literature to be found, and even fewer people to talk to it about," he explains. "There were a few people, of course, but most of my writing friends—even those I now see in person regularly—I first met online."[1]

In sharing the books he has read, Bell aims to connect with fellow readers with similar interests, while perhaps exposing little-known writers and publishers he thinks need attention. "It's also a way for me to suggest that people check some of those books out, without being pushy. My tastes run toward the unconventional and the indie presses," he says.

Bell posts his reading list to his Web site and then takes it a step further by sharing his current reading online via social media, with sites such as Facebook. There, he also offers inspirational quotes from writers which start off his own day's creative activities. "I work at home from my desk a lot of my day. There are a lot of fun and interesting people on there, both my friends and family and the larger communities of writers and readers

---

[1]Originally interviewed by Lori A. May, for "Get involved: Play an active part in the writing community." *The Writer*, May 2010.

I've found myself a part of," he says. "Mostly I'm just excited to be in contact with a lot of other people interested in the same things as me. And Facebook certainly provides that."

Regardless of where a writer or reader lives, the internet allows and encourages such interaction. Sharing books you love, authors you've discovered, or literary events taking place in your area is a great way to connect with others and perhaps even turn another reader onto something that reader wouldn't have discovered on his or her own. More significant, as Bell touches on, are the connections that may be made from one reader to another. Writers and readers who live in remote areas without local access to in-person communities can find themselves a part of a literary conversation with others from around the world.

"Many writers whom I would name as vital members of my writing community I haven't yet met in person," says author Gale Martin. "Somehow, their influence and support have been keenly felt and appreciated, thanks to technology."

It's not just connecting with others through one-on-one discussions, either, that Martin appreciates. "You can host a radio show on Blogtalk or some similar such avenue and feature a writer friend," she says. "You can do a video review or read a chapter and post it on YouTube. Or if you don't have much time, you can simply retweet their Tweets or share their Facebook posts with your friends."

Sharing the successes and news of other writers is a great way to feel a part of the global literary conversation. The time commitment is variable and customizable, too. Sharing news and links through social media takes little time and effort. Yet, there are countless opportunities for focusing a bit more time in shining the spotlight on others.

New York Times' bestselling children's author Debbie Diesen runs a series on her blog that specifically features other writers. "Michigander Monday" is a weekly profile series in which the author does a Q&A with writers hailing from her home state. "I'd met or learned about so many wonderful, talented, good-hearted children's book authors and illustrators living in my home state of Michigan, I wanted to do my small part to make more people aware of their fabulous books," Diesen says, though she long ago broadened her scope to include writers in all genres. "I also hoped the feature might help highlight the collective abundance of writing talent that Michigan has. Michigan may not be known widely as a literary hotspot, but I genuinely believe it should be."

To ease her time commitment, the author uses a preselected list of questions she shares with writers who then respond via email at their leisure. Diesen says "it's a very manageable expenditure of time. . . . I've loved every interview I've done and have learned something new from every author I've featured. Above all, the Michigander Monday feature helps me feel and stay connected to the writing community, a place where I am ever thankful and grateful to belong." Her process is a win-win for both parties, and for readers, as Diesen shares writers of all experiences and all genres, while sharing links to their books and Web sites.

"If you help get someone excited about a book," Diesen says, "if you help connect a reader to an author, you're benefiting not just that author and that book and that reader. In a small way, you're benefiting the entire literary community. So I guess that's what I hope to accomplish with the feature. To, in some small way, widen the world."

To add to the reader's experience, Diesen only focuses half the interview on the author's writing; the rest of the Q&A includes the interviewee's favorite places to visit in Michigan, including bookstores and libraries, other cultural events, and also asks the featured author to share a few recommended authors others should know about. In doing so, there is a continual loop of literary citizenship in sharing books, writers, and locales that may interest readers.

What Diesen, Bell, and others are doing with the internet may be accomplished by any reader, any writer, in areas populated or remote. Connecting with others in person in your local community is a great way to build a "literary borough," yet when that doesn't seem possible, building an online community may help you connect with like-minded readers and contribute your interests, skills, and passion to a more global literary conversation.

5

From the Editor's Desk

This is not a marketing guide. Becoming a more engaged literary citizen will not catapult you to fame and fortune; it will not guarantee that your books are published—or that when they do, they become bestsellers. The intention of this book is not to show you ways to network and schmooze with others. The purpose of this book is to share authentic ways by which we can connect with others who share a love of literature and who wish to celebrate what other writers are doing.

That being said, perhaps you're a skeptic. Maybe you need an incentive to know that getting involved and contributing to the bigger picture is worth your time. You might wonder if your efforts would even be noticed among a sea of others already doing their part.

The truth is maybe only a few people will notice. Perhaps only one or two others will be affected by your contribution to the community. But there's nothing wrong with or disappointing in that; literary citizenship is about quality, not quantity. Remember the discussion in Chapter 1, about what not to expect from literary citizenship? Giving something back to the community for the sake of contributing will undoubtedly enrich your own life and your own artistry. The mere pleasure of getting involved and being in touch with others should be its own reward.

However, for those who need a little more motivation, a little confirmation that being a working part of the whole matters, this chapter is for you. Here, a handful of editors and agents weigh in on why community involvement is important and why these qualities are also at times a contributing factor they look at when considering potential authors.

Literary citizenship may not make or break a book contract, but the reality is editors and agents want to see writers who step outside of the isolated box of creativity and into the community. Yes, in doing so, an author positions himself or herself to network, promote, and market his or her own work, but the following editors and agents agree that *engagement* with the community is far more valuable than a robotic ability to sell one's work. In-person conversations will run short if one party only has his or her personal platform to promote and not spare a moment to converse with others. Likewise, no one is impressed with an author's monotone self-promotion on Twitter or Facebook. Copying and pasting your book link every day may, in fact, have the opposite effect intended. Rather, it is those who reach beyond themselves and their work to authentically communicate within the community that appeals not only to editors and agents, but— more importantly—also to peers and readers. Connecting with others matters. Let's look at why.

Kate Gale, publisher of Red Hen Press, shares this story of when she was introduced to a writer who seemed like a potential fit for the publishing house. "One of my writers asked me to meet with someone who was hoping to become a Red Hen writer. I knew the work was good, so I agreed to meet with this writer at AWP. When I ran into her, she was speaking to another writer I know and respect, so it was very clear she was in my circle and this was promising. We met for an hour to talk about whether Red Hen should publish her book, but at the end of the hour I knew the answer was no," says Gale. Why? "The conversation was all about what I could do for her and how my work could support hers. She brought nothing to the table."

Red Hen Press was founded with Gale's own investment: her passion, time, energy, and money. It's important to her that the authors she brings onto the team feel equally invested in others. What does that mean?

"I'd like an author who's going to be engaged in the world on more than one level," she says. "Our authors who have been successful are those who get out in the world and travel for events, engage with readers. In some ways that's easier to do if you offer to do things, like offer a workshop, set up your own reading or a reading series, etc."

The writing, Gale says, is always the first priority. But if an author isn't interested in stepping out from behind the writing desk, it can be a deal-breaker for the publisher. An author who demonstrates interest in the community, by engaging with readers through a variety of channels and by supporting what others are doing, carries that much more weight.

Agent Andrea Hurst agrees. "No matter what our differences may be, when you are a writer, you're a part of a family." As the president of Andrea Hurst & Associates, the agent advocates that writers find as many ways as possible to support the literary work of others. "It is important that we keep the whole process going from writing to selling and buying books," she says. "Each time you help a writer, buy a book, or take a class you are not only obtaining benefit for yourself but for everyone involved from author to agent to publisher."[1]

When Hurst is considering adding a potential client to those she represents, she looks at the author's overall engagement within the publishing ecosystem. "We want writers who are involved in polishing their craft, active in publishing communities, and open to learning new things."

While editors and agents may be focused on the sales and promotional skills a writer may bring to the table, an active participation within the greater community can often indicate whether a writer is comfortable reaching out to an audience. Kevin Morgan Watson, publisher and editor of Press 53 in Winston-Salem, says their ideal author is "personable, likable, and professional, and knows how to connect with his or her readers."

Press 53 expects to see writers with "lots of publication credits to show they are active and building a support team of editors and other writers who can help get word out about their book," yet seeing one's work in print is not enough on its

---

[1]Originally interviewed by Lori A. May, for "Get involved: Play an active part in the writing community." *The Writer*, May 2010.

own. The publisher adds, "Authors today can't rely on reviews and bookstores to reach their readers; an author has to think outside the old models and connect with readers on social media, by giving readings to community groups, professional organizations, book clubs, Friends of the Library events, literary festivals, and so on."

These acts of cultural engagement—connecting with readers and fellow writers—are indeed ways to expand one's marketing platform, yet they are also an opportunity to connect in more meaningful ways. It takes the same amount of time and effort to cheer on a fellow writer's work as it does to promote one's own interests. In thinking beyond one's sales efforts, a writer can multi-task the practical side of publishing *and* have an impact on one's local community.

We have all met at least one or two (or more) writers who seem to be walking billboards, constantly promoting their latest book. On social media, how many times have you scrolled by the news feed of a writer who only ever talks about himself or herself? Yet, there are writers who seamlessly marry the necessity to occasionally self-promote with their genuine and greater interest in connecting with others as fellow humans. These authors may discuss their latest reads, personal travels, or other hobbies and interests. They talk about more than writing and publishing. They are real people with real quirks, curiosities, and passions. These are the authors we are drawn to, are they not?

These are also the authors who share good news from others, promote a friend's new release, and help connect other like-minded readers and writers. What makes their efforts stand out from those who only promote their own works? That's simple. The writers who successfully share their personal good news do so when necessary, when a new release is available, and when they have something to share with potential readers. Yet, watch these writers on social media and at in-person events; you'll see how their time dedicated to a personal platform is minimal in comparison with what else they offer to others: a steady source of inspiration, motivation, and camaraderie that exists apart from their self-serving needs.

Marie Gauthier, director of sales and marketing at Tupelo Press, encourages authors to be active on and offline. "Everyone has different comfort levels, but I hope to see authors having fun on Facebook, Tweeting, talking up other authors, and being a vocal and supportive presence at literary events, including those in their local communities," she says. "The internet has expanded the size and reach of the literary community, but it needn't be at the expense of the literary culture of the town you live in. The proprietor of the local bed and breakfast that lodges the poets your reading series brings to the café around the corner buys poetry books, too. Literary citizenship means contributing to the health and vibrancy of our literary culture through whatever means you're able. . . . There is no end of ways you can add to the conversation and foster a readership."

Making real connections

Veronica Windholz, an editor at Penguin, says editors seek the same community-minded qualities in writers that others do; that is, "authors who are already 'leaders' of one sort or another—around whom others want to congregate because of their effectiveness in reaching out, through empathy and in empathy, to other human beings."

In her profession, Windholz edits books acquired by her colleagues, but she is also very much engaged with authors and through her Web site, OnCloseReading.com, where she offers her time to share practical advice about writing, revising, and storytelling. Her efforts as a literary citizen are aimed at improving the writer's writing, as this is where she finds her strongest connection.

"Good writing is about connecting with people in places where they didn't even know they needed to feel a connection," she says. "The most successful and effective authors draw their audiences in, creating a powerful community of like-minded souls."

Windholz acknowledges that authors are most comfortable on the page, but "all of them love to connect, to reach out, to make a difference—and all of them love to be appreciated. It's a virtuous circle of the most nourishing kind."

It's that sense of belonging in a grounded community that is at the heart of literary citizenship. Too, engagement with others doesn't always have to be focused on the act of writing itself. It is how the writing unites us that matters. Remember how author Loreen Niewenhuis worked to find ways to connect with others who shared her passion for the Great Lakes? Sometimes our writing and our books are mere tools to connect us with others, as Windholz suggests.

As writers, we have something to say. We choose to pick up the pen or sit in front of our computer for a reason. We want our words to be read and for our thoughts to be understood in some way. As readers, we're thrilled to experience that flutter of connection when an author expresses something we've thought, just so, in the words that we perhaps weren't sure how to express ourselves. Writing inspires connection.

Katherine Sears, cofounder of Booktrope Publishing, reiterates this thought. "Authors tend to write about things they are passionate about," she says. If the books reach the right readers, she adds, "a good portion of their efforts will allow them to highlight and showcase their passions whether that be for writing, or for cooking, or the romantic nature of the human condition. Even the lightest of fiction offerings serve a meaningful purpose. They entertain and allow us to step out of our lives for a time. I can't think of anything more meaningful than that!"

Sears says Booktrope works only with those authors who branch out of their writing life to connect with others. Their publishing team values what authors can give of themselves to their immediate readership, but also to the greater community. The concept of literary citizenship, she says, "makes me think of something my father always taught us about being stewards of the land. He felt that if we spent time in the outdoors, camping, hiking, etc, that it was our responsibility to not just leave things as we found them, but better than we found them. As a result, I grew up picking up other people's trash on walks, leaving things better than I found them."

As Booktrope Publishing was founded on the idea of team-work and collaboration, where authors hand-select their respective marketing, editing, and design partners, Sears values the effort each individual puts into the bigger picture. "So, much like my father's passion for the improvement of the environment, we want to change the nature of publishing for the better," she says. "We hope that we are encouraging respectful and collaborative behavior in our authors and other community members."

The idea of collaboration and community *within* a publishing house is not new, but it's certainly regaining momentum, particularly with smaller independent and nonprofit presses. Betsy Teter, the executive director of Hub City in Spartanburg SC, explains how the community outreach of their Hub City Writers Project aligns with their press through sometimes unpredictable means. "About a decade ago, a local writer named Michel Stone came to our summer conference called Writing in Place, which we have sponsored at Wofford for thirteen years now," she says. "An in-class assignment during those three days led to a short story. The next year Michel submitted her story to our annual Upstate creative writing contest. She won, and the prize was a week at Wildacres Writers Workshop."

While at the intensive writing workshop, the winning author took her short story idea and expanded it into a novel. "When she was finished, she submitted it to the SC First Novel Competition, which we sponsor with the SC Arts Commission. It didn't win," Teter says, "but one of our first readers was so enthralled with it, the Hub City editorial board recommended its publication." *The Iguana Tree* was subsequently published, but even more

who the author is—and for our contest, the reading is done without author names—and choose based on literary merit. But we hope for this kind of author, and when we get to the point with an author where we are discussing taking on their book, we make our expectations for their engagement with the literary community clear."

So, what is it that Rose Metal Press hopes to find in a potential author? "We encourage our authors to cultivate some form of an active online presence," Rooney says, but "within that presence, we also look for someone who seems to be interested not merely in sharing information about themselves and their projects, but also in mentioning, discussing, commenting on, and reviewing work by other writers and artists."

Rooney adds that there is no downside for writers to cultivate a presence in the community. "As far as giving back goes, it's hard to be interesting if you are not also interested," she says. "If a writer finds it too much additional work to read and review or interview or encourage other writers, that writer might need to alter his or her definition of 'additional work' and realize that that kind of other-directed interest is—or should be—part of wanting to be a writer in the first place."

One way the founders of Rose Metal Press encourage literary citizenship is to ask their writers to give what they have themselves received. "We ask our authors to think of all the people who took the time to read their book and review it, to interview them, or mention their book. In the current small press world where so many reviewers, bloggers, website developers and moderators, publishers, and editors work for very little or no compensation to build and expand a vibrant literary landscape, the good old karmic golden rule applies."

The founders argue that this is about paying kindness forward and reminding authors of the valuable time others give in recommending books. Rooney and Beckel hope to see their authors take the same time, the same care, to contribute something back to the writing community.

"It meant a lot to you as an author every time someone else took the time to read your book and respond to it, so why not take the time to read, review, rate, or otherwise offer feedback on someone else's book? We don't view or suggest this in a 'you scratch my back, I'll scratch yours' way," Rooney adds, "but in a pay it forward and build the community way of taking time for other writers' work the way others in the community have taken time for yours."

We all feel the same when our work is appreciated by another. We're moved, humbled, perhaps relieved, and—in some ways—validated, when our writing is actually being read and enjoyed by others. Offering a few moments of your time to spread the news of another writer's new release, or reviewing a new book that you feel passionate about, is a simple way to give something back and to ensure another writer feels that moment of satisfaction in having his or her work appreciated.

For the skeptics out there, for those who may consider all of these aspects of community outreach to be time consuming or perhaps a distraction from the writing, rest assured it is the writing that must always come first. A writer must first and foremost write a compelling book or an engaging story. As Penguin editor Veronica Windholz said, it's the human quality within the writing that draws in the reader.

Literary agent Albert LaFarge adds that no amount of community outreach is going to turn an average writer into a blockbuster success. "Visibility doesn't always translate into interest in books," he says, "and the most important thing for me to see in a writer is the ability to find a good story or subject and relate it in a convincing, appealing way. Good stories have a way of creating audiences."

These agents and editors have shared why they value a stable of authors who are invested in their communities. It's not merely about marketing and book sales. It's about developing a rapport with like-minded readers and finding common grounds on which to connect.

In connecting with those audiences via social media, in reaching out to other writers, and in offering more of your presence than in touting one's book, a greater sense of community can enhance a writer's life.

Making authentic choices

Literary citizenship, like writing, must come from an authentic place within the writer. It must come from a true desire to be a part of the literary ecosystem.

Author Matt Bell says "there's no doubt that doing all of these things has had a tangible effect on my available opportunities, when seen over a long enough period of time. But that's not why

I do any of it, and I can't advocate people doing these things because they'll get something in return. That will ruin almost all of these events and experiences, and has for others."

Authentic community engagement should offer its own reward in the sense of contributing to something outside of one's self. In helping other authors, emerging and established alike, there is joy to be had in celebrating others' successes and sharing new work that excites us, and that we believe will excite others. It is also through our interactions with others that we expand our knowledge, challenge our views, and stimulate our creative minds by being inspired by others and their works.

"I review books or blog about work I like or think is important because I want other people to read it and enjoy it, too," Bell says. "Those are the kinds of reasons that make something worth doing, and really, writers should be doing this stuff anyway, in some combination that works for them. That's living the literary life."

Sure, editors and agents want to see their authors be active within the community. For those of you skeptics who need a little more motivation than the simple joy of connecting with others and doing good for good's sake, perhaps the comments from those above will motivate you to look at how you can contribute to the literary community. But, as most everyone above has mentioned, you will want to find ways to get involved that are authentic to you and in tune with your particular interests. The purpose of literary citizenship is to open up the possibilities for creating a more fulfilling life—for you and for others.

6

Book Reviewing: Write (about) What you Read

Book reviewing is arguably one of the easiest forms of literary citizenship. There is no long-term commitment—unless that's what you seek—and there is no need to leave the comfort of your writing desk. A reviewer need only read with attention and respond to the work with care. To demonstrate this effectively, four examples of published book reviews are included as an appendix at the end of this book. As Joe Ponepinto, former book review editor for the *Los Angeles Review*, says, "Book reviewing is definitely one of the most expedient ways to become involved in the literary community, since reviewers are always in demand, and reviews don't necessarily require the imagination of a short story, poem, or creative nonfiction."

Book lovers of all genres look to reviews to make purchase decisions, find recommendations for themselves and others, and to round out their awareness of what's being published. Informal reviews posted in online retail environments may be brief, but they are not always trusted by potential buyers due to the lack of editorial vetting. Indeed, quality book reviews do benefit from a skilled editor's eye; and, while each review venue has a unique esthetic, review editors are most often concerned with fairly and accurately interpreting the work up for discussion.

Zach Savich, one of the book review editors at *The Kenyon Review*, says "I hope that the reviews we publish in *The Kenyon Review* and *KROnline* consequentially affect how readers think about contemporary literature. Yes, one function of a review is somewhat heraldic—to announce new work, to bring attention to titles that readers might otherwise miss, to help a reader decide if a book might be right for her—or to give her the ability to discuss its significance, even if she never reads it. But reviews also impact readers' wider thinking about literature, and, in a magazine like *KR*," Savich says, "their commentary inflects the poetry, fiction, nonfiction, and drama alongside which they are published. *KR* provides our reviewers with a venue from which to contribute to this process and to the conversations it inspires. Each year, we are able to review only a small number of the books I wish we could. I'm grateful to the reviewers whose good work, along with the books they write about, become part of the larger *KR* community."

Writing a book review needn't be time consuming. Most publications publish reviews ranging from 500 to 1,000 words, though there are a few journals that occasionally seek more extensive pieces. Yet with such a focused word count and ample opportunities to publish reviews in literary journals and in online venues, many writers find it's a reasonable goal to commit to reviewing two or three titles a year. Most writers and devoted readers take in far more than this for pleasure; dedicating a couple of days to compose a meaningful response to the work can make a lasting impact on the reviewed author and, most importantly, for other readers.

Paying it forward

There is an unfortunate disconnect between the abundance of books being published and the quantity of reviews coming from the literary community. "To be plain, it's frustrating that everybody wants to be reviewed, but few people seem to want to write reviews," says Alex Boyd, editor of *Northern Poetry Review*. "When there's shrinking media attention for books, and the media has a tendency to go to the same people for comment, every little bit helps."

I've personally heard a sampling of authors say that they steer clear of book reviewing, as there is a concern that doing so tarnishes the writing community and that reviewing another author's work is treading in dangerous waters. In fact, at a writing conference I attended recently, there was a panel discussion about reviewing and a few audience members debated whether reviewing was somehow on a par with "peeing in one's own pool."

Others, still, argued that the process made them feel "dirty," as though offering critical commentary on published books should be reserved for another breed of writers—just not literary types.

Thankfully, other writers raised hands to counter these arguments, claiming that reviewing books allows them to contribute to a larger literary conversation and, yes, support the work of their fellows. As Boyd states plainly above, there has been a drastic decline in reviews being published—particularly in newspapers—and it has largely become the responsibility of those truly invested in sharing recommendations to seek venues for critical commentary.

As published writers, we hope our books make a connection with readers and there is no greater proof of that than in reading a reader's response in a review, regardless of length, regardless of venue. A few words expressing the reader's reaction, and his take on the execution of craft and language, can do wonders to lift a writer's spirits *and* help expose a new book to more readers.

Yet, some writers are cautious, saying they shy away from reviewing as they don't want to be put in the position of saying something critical of another's work. To this, author Wayne Ude urges a fair handling of criticism to ensure an authentic contribution to the literary dialogue. "Literary citizenship should mean behaving decently and honestly in our relations with other writers. Reviews of, or even comments about, other writers and their work must be honest. If the work has problems, say so, but also praise when appropriate."

Book reviewing is, in its own right, a professional form of writing and handling one's self as a professional is the key to offering a thoughtful critical analysis. That means critically assessing the good with the not so good. Ude argues that "so long as the negative evaluations are honestly arrived at, the author needs to recognize that negative reviews are part of the world she or he has entered."

The fringe benefits of reviewing

Reviewing books on a regular basis generally means a writer is also reading new work with regularity. Not only does offering a review help contribute to the global conversation of literature, but also the process of discovering and analyzing books can, in and of itself, offer a value to the reviewer.

"Reviewing books has given me a clear indication of what different presses are publishing," says Brian Fanelli, author of *Front Man*. "The poetry world is so vast right now, with so many different styles happening. Reviewing has allowed me to sample those different styles and develop a clear understanding of the type of poetry associated with various presses and publishers. This is especially useful to me as a writer who is constantly submitting work. Furthermore, it has connected me to other writers through Facebook and other social media outlets."

In my own activities as a reviewer, I have often connected with readers who stumbled upon my reviews and wanted to touch base to thank me for sharing new work. I've also heard from some of the authors of books I have reviewed who reach out to offer thanks, but that's not the reason I review. I do so as

I feel the inclination to share reading recommendations and to participate in the community on this level. Yet, there is no greater feeling than hearing from readers and writers who appreciated a review I wrote. It lets me know I struck a chord with a fellow book lover.

Similarly, author Leslie Nielsen contributes to review publications, such as *Poets' Quarterly*, for the connection she feels with peers. "Reading submitted work and working with writers is so incredibly gratifying," she says. "The bigger context is that it's always been hugely important to me to be involved in whatever community I'm part of."

As the blog and essays editor of *Poets' Quarterly*, Nielsen not only reviews, but also engages in conversations about literature with writers of various experiences. "I love the reviews we publish. They feel a little bit like the work-room of our establishment, and the interviews feel like training seminars. In some ways I hope the essays section is like a lounge where conversations flow on all levels from the raucous or purely pleasurable to those fantastic deep and probing talks after-hours."

It's her ability to connect with like-minded peers that keeps Nielsen motivated and connected with the community. "I ran a visiting writer series once and on all the promo it said, 'Without community, we perish, and all our fine words with us.' That's a little stark, but not overstated. Writing is solitary, but we all crave and thrive on vital community to propel that effort. *PQ* seems especially well structured to provide that community."

Other writers find that reviewing new books is a way to inform craft and propel creativity to new and unchartered territory.

As an example, FeLicia Elam is a fiction writer, yet she reviews poetry books as a way to appreciate what she finds to be a more intimidating genre. "Writing reviews actually makes poetry more approachable and exercises my 'poetry brain,'" she says. "Writing reviews helps me become more daring with my own work. When I see an author take a risk or combining techniques, I contemplate whether or not their technique is something I can incorporate into my practice. Writing poetry reviews allows me another way to study poetry, another way to discover poets, and another connection into the writing community."

The benefits of reviewing, then, are layered. A reviewer shares recommended reading with a hungry audience, exposing a worthy book in need of attention, while also exercising one's craft skills in absorbing what others are doing and possibly considering how to push the boundaries of one's own craft.

The basics of breaking in

For those interested in reviewing and contributing to the literary conversation, how does one proceed? Start small. Share a brief review on your blog or on a fellow writer's Web site. Offer up a few words in the comment sections of online retailers, where potential book buyers will see your recommendations. Most importantly, *read* reviews. In exploring what journals publish reviews and determining their individual esthetics, you'll discover where you might like to query or submit an on-spec review and where your particular writing style may fit best.

Most journals that publish reviews are in steady need of contributors. As these opportunities are dominantly of a volunteer nature, writers come and go depending on their own personal and professional commitments. Joe Ponepinto says, "As a review editor I try, whenever possible, to give writers the opportunity to prove themselves as reviewers, but I have to balance that with my responsibility to readers to provide a fair and professional assessment of the works in question. That commitment to readers takes precedence."

Ponepinto says that when he edited with *Los Angeles Review*, he hoped to find writers who were "able to discuss the book in terms not only of its entertainment value, but also of its place in literature and what it brings to the larger culture—and I make that clear to every reviewer before they start."

The query process for book reviewing is quite simple. Some publications consider on-spec reviews, where a writer sends in a completed piece for consideration, whereas other journals prefer to assign books for review. Alyse Bensel, current editor with *Los Angeles Review*, says "prospective reviewers should introduce themselves, provide a brief overview of the title and tell the editor why the potential review is important for this particular publication—for example, if poems or stories were previously published in that journal." Bensel says interested editors tend to follow up within a week or two, though she suggests that writers are "patient and courteous" during the query process.

The most basic query letter can be successful. Essentially, a brief note introducing yourself and your review interests will give an editor all he needs to know. Using *Poets' Quarterly* as an example, a successful query letter may read along these lines:

Dear Andrew,

Would you be interested in a 700-word review of *The Plath Cabinet* by Catherine Bowman (Four Way Books)? I'm an emerging writer based in Petal MS and it would be my pleasure to contribute to *Poets' Quarterly*.

Thank you for your consideration,
Alice Playwright

If you're an experienced reviewer, you might also share your past publications, as in this sample query directed to *Los Angeles Review*:

Dear Alyse Bensel,

My name is Daniel Pecchenino, and I teach in the Writing Program at USC. I finished up my PhD in English at UCSB a couple years ago, and I am looking for opportunities to write more book reviews, having done so in the past for *American Literature* and *Flaunt*. Are there any openings at the *Los Angeles Review* at this time? I actually have a poem coming out in issue 14 of *LAR*, and am a big fan of what your publication does. Thank you, and I hope this note finds you well.

All best,
Daniel Pecchenino

Thanks to this query, Pecchenino became a reviewer—and eventually an assistant book review editor—for *Los Angeles Review*.

You'll want to study the individual query and submission guidelines for any publication you wish to submit, but the process is often straightforward and welcoming. Dan Beachy-Quick, book reviews editor for *Colorado Review*, directs prospective reviewers to use the contact email or submission system literary journals list on their main Web site. "A reviewer need not have any experience writing reviews," he adds, "though should pay good attention to the style sheet I send with my response to the query." Alyse Bensel adds that novice reviewers "may need to send a sample of your writing in order to confirm you are capable of writing a review. Having samples on hand is a must."

Sample material is as easy as posting brief reviews on your personal blog or on bookseller sites like Powell's. Approaching a review for the first time, though, can be a little intimidating. It's not only the stylistic approach a reviewer must consider, but also what the reviewer can bring to the table that's unique to her reading experience that will ensure a stand-out review. "As with writing a poem, one has to find a voice," says Beachy-Quick. "The book review—the good book review, that is—also feels to me an aesthetic effort. Find examples that interest, even *matter*, to you. Begin with imitation until the idiosyncrasy of your own thinking finds expression. Write about books you admire, or better, find out—maybe in the process of writing the review itself—that you love."

The art of critical review

Reading, analyzing, and emulating published reviews can be helpful for those starting out and that is why a few samples have been included in this book as an appendix.

One of the review authors, Dr Jacqueline Lyons, also an assistant professor of English at California Lutheran University, suggests that one's personal review style will develop over time as different approaches lead to a more refined esthetic. "When writing my first reviews of poetry books I focused on a combination of micro and macro views," she says. "I tried to characterize the collection and describe the arc of the book, as well as close read each poem and thoroughly research references. While still close reading selected poems and noticing the book's progression, my approach has evolved into the review as an essay, with an arc of its own, intended to preview the book for potential readers. I see the review as an opportunity to present and promote poetry. Rather than judging the book, I think of my reviews as introductions: if a book sounds compelling, then readers will want to have their own conversation with it."

Lyons's review of Brian Teare's *Companion Grasses* was originally published in *Colorado Review* and editor Dan Beachy-Quick says this piece demonstrates much of what he admires in a review: "a sense of language that isn't so much a comment on style as it is a window into the deeper work the poetry is trying to accomplish. That deeper work needs to be made apprehensible to the reader of the review. . . . The review limns the necessary themes of the book, not as an argument, but as an enticement to the reader that promises to leave the experience of reading intact for whoever might go and buy it."

One of the most common mistakes in reviewing is in summarizing too much while leaving out an analytical component. Newcomers to the genre may find the Purdue Online Writing Lab[1] helpful for its step-by-step list of points to consider in reviewing. However, many publications, such as *Los Angeles Review*, have a preferred personalized approach for writing reviews.

"I'm always looking for critical engagement with the text that does not solely rely on summary," says *Los Angeles Review* editor Alyse Bensel. "Reviewers should be able to discuss what the text is doing and highlight the writing from that text. Reviews are not the reviewer's unfounded personal opinion of the text; rather, reviews use evidence from the text to support any claim made about that text. Staying on what the text is doing instead of what it did not do is integral to effective reviews. This doesn't mean I'm against 'negative' reviews, but I want to see reviews that actually use evidence from the text when making a critique."

As an example, Bensel says the two reviews included in the appendix written by B. J. Hollars provide "a brief but effective overview of the book and then goes into interpreting what he thinks the title is doing. He then goes on to provide specific evidence from particular stories or excerpts that best demonstrate what he's claiming. The language of the review is direct, easy to follow, and accessible for our readers."

---

[1]Purdue Online Writing Lab: https://owl.english.purdue.edu/owl/resource/704/1/.

Editors like Bensel and Beachy-Quick encourage new reviewers to consider each publication's individual editorial policies and published pieces to get a true idea of how to approach a submission. Writers will want to ensure that the style is appropriate and on a par with past published reviews, and that the word count and house style guidelines are followed accurately.

Beyond the basics, Bensel says a good reviewer knows that the successful publication of a review is not the end point, but the start of a conversation—with readers and with editors. "Once your review comes out, help promote that publication through social media or by telling people you know," she says. "Follow up with the editor about writing additional reviews or if you plan on not reviewing for that publication anymore. You don't want to be the reviewer who promises several reviews and never writes them. Rather, you want to be reliable, consistent, and pleasant to work with."

Beyond reviewing

While it's certainly beneficial to write reviews for publications and gain an audience that appreciates one's reviews, journal editors want to see authentic critical analysis that focuses on the work being reviewed, not on the reviewer and his personal agenda.

"I worry that [reviewing] is often seen careeristically," says editor Zach Savich. "It's easy to tell when a potential reviewer cares more about adding *The Kenyon Review* to their publication credits, or flattering an author under review, than about writing a thoughtful piece."

His concern is that writers confuse the intent of literary citizenship with a means to self-market. "Such promotion can be beautiful. I am grateful to so many people who run readings series, presses, magazines, organizations that connect writing to varied communities, and so forth. They add value to my life every day," he says. "But I also know that there can be an exhausting, obsessive culture of self-promotion and of the voluble promotion of one's friends that can, at times, prevent other expressions of literary citizenship, including those that would be more private or meaningfully connected to seemingly nonliterary communities."

Yet, finding a home to publish your reviews may eventually open up further opportunities to get involved in supporting the community. Whether that's helping a journal during the bookfair at a conference like AWP or in other avenues of building readership, there are sometimes additional and perhaps lesser-known avenues to extend your support.

Savich has been involved with *Kenyon Review* since 2008, when he first wrote reviews for the magazine. Since then, he has worked as a book review editor and as a consulting editor, and has also taught in *KR*'s Young Writers Workshop, an intensive summer program for high school writers. He says that "although *KR* has been central to the last years of my life as a writer, I still frequently learn about additional aspects of *KR*'s lively, dynamic programming." These include a postgraduate fellowship program, a major award for literary achievement, community literacy initiatives, a yearly literary festival, and creative writing workshops for adults, teachers, and teens.

"I'm not directly involved with most of *KR*'s programs," Savich says, "but I'm proud to be part of the vision of literary community that these programs advance, which is principled, inclusive, and continually changing to connect the life of literature to new audiences. I hope the work we do with book reviews—through the titles we review, through the quality of our reviewers' work—supports those goals."

Writers and readers seeking a low-commitment way to contribute to the literary community may find book reviewing to be a manageable venture. Writing a few reviews a year can enhance one's own appreciation of craft while also reaching out to like-minded readers. For those with an interest in contributing even more time and energy to sharing worthy reading recommendations, we'll now take a look at additional opportunities to explore in working with journals and small presses.

7

In Print and Online: Working with Presses and Journals

A quick scan through databases compiled by Duotrope, New-Pages, and other submission resources will demonstrate the diversity, breadth, and sheer number of literary journals and presses operating today. Many of these are independent start-ups that rely on volunteers to run day-to-day tasks, while others are supported by academic institutions or nonprofit agencies. While the number of presses and journals may be intimidating for a writer seeking the right venue for a publication, the good news is there are countless opportunities for literary citizens. How so? Most small presses and journals count on dedicated team members who are willing to offer a few hours a month to help read submissions, organize fundraising campaigns, and promote new publications.

What's wonderful about our digital age is that geography is of little concern. A writer in a remote area may find himself or herself working as a first reader or editor with an urban publication; conversely, a city dweller may enjoy collaborating with a publication from a laid-back rural town. Across the nation, and internationally as well, publishers and managing editors rely on skilled, creative, and invested volunteers who are willing to make a contribution of time and effort in carrying out their mission.

Working with a press can be a rewarding experience on multiple levels. First and foremost is the gratification of working with peers who aim to select and share new work with readers. Secondly, your involvement may open up doors to meeting new people and this can complement an otherwise solitary writing life. "Co-editing *PANK* and blogging for *HTMLGIANT* have really helped me to connect to other writers, editors, and readers," says Roxane Gay. That connection, and the rapport built with readers, can add up to a greater sense of belonging within the writing community.

In my own various volunteer roles with small presses, I have had similar experiences. In reading others' work, in connecting readers with new writing, and in communicating with editors and contributors at national conferences and in online conversations, I have seen my community blossom in ways I didn't imagine possible. Those connections have made a lasting impact in widening my circle of peers, and they have most certainly influenced what I include in my regular activity as a literary citizen. Even in my busiest hours as a writer, I reserve a bit of my time for working with others in an editorial capacity. My involvement with journals and presses keeps me connected, motivated, and inspired beyond my own writing ambitions.

Matt Bell, editor at *The Collagist*, says serving as an editor of literary magazines is "a part of my literary life that's almost as important to me as my own writing. Editing is an opportunity to engage deeply with other writers, and to encourage and promote writers whose work I see as important and innovative. The process of doing so—reading submissions, accepting work, editing with the writers, publishing and promoting the issues— is some of the most enjoyable and personally meaningful work I've ever done."

Learning from experience

We've all heard the advice given to emerging writers: Read literary journals. Submit your work. And, yes, help out at a journal or small press to learn the other side of publishing. That's because the experience of reviewing incoming submissions, reading query letters, and learning the ins and outs of how editors select work to showcase is a valuable lesson for writers. It can prompt us to improve our craft and add an additional level of professionalism in how we interact with editors.

Jessie Carty, editor of *Referential Magazine*, expresses how editing has been an important learning tool for her writing. "I wish I'd worked on a magazine earlier in my writing life. Working the other side of the desk, I think, can make you much more compassionate for editors in general, and gives you a new insight into what is going on in the contemporary writing world—the good and the bad."

Carty says that working as an editor is a way to support writers whose work she enjoys, but the routine editorial tasks have made her take a closer look at her own writing and submissions. "I don't want to be rejected by someone simply because I made grammatical errors, or didn't follow submission guidelines. On a deeper level, I also start looking for more clichéd images and phrasing," she says, "because that tends to be what I find myself rejecting most often. I want to read something I haven't read before."

Leslie Nielsen, an editor with *Poets' Quarterly* and other venues, adds an additional benefit to volunteering. "There's a self-serving face to the job, and a hope that if I volunteer well, I'll progress on the wished-for path to a paid gig somewhere. It's like credentialing and hoping some people come to recognize my name and skills."

Indeed, for writers and readers who wish to develop a career in publishing, there is no greater learning experience than volunteering with a variety of publications.

Realizing a vision

You might be considering starting your own journal or small press. With Web platforms becoming more and more user-friendly, an online journal requires very little time and money upfront, yet doing so still requires a long-term vision and a clear mission. Spending some time volunteering with experienced peers can help hone your skills and demonstrate how to develop your idea into a reality.

Those who have embraced the challenge to start a journal have often done so to fill a void they saw in the market. Donna Talarico, publisher of *Hippocampus Magazine*, did exactly that when she "recognized a gap in online magazines that focused solely on creative nonfiction. There are so many that accept poetry or fiction, or poetry *and* fiction. I wanted to create a place for writers like me."

Likewise, while there is an abundance of independent presses populating the market, there is ample room to explore unique mandates in book publishing. Kaylie Jones, author of *A Soldier's Daughter Never Cries* and *Lies My Mother Never Told Me*, felt frustrated when she would come upon promising manuscripts that weren't catching the eyes of the mainstream book publishers. "For a long time I've felt powerless to take the writing projects I've mentored, or come across through colleagues, to the next level—publishing," she says. "Even the yearly $10,000 James Jones Literary Society First Novel Fellowship only helps a novel get some attention. It doesn't guarantee publication."

So Jones took action. "Waking up in despair one morning, I decided to try my hand at an imprint. I approached Johnny Temple, publisher of Akashic Books, with this idea," she says, "and he and his staff, whom I've known for years, were very enthusiastic." The author knew this was the right place for her to begin an imprint, as she has "felt deeply connected to their mission and their general disinterest in the more commercial aspects of mainstream publishing."

The mission of Kaylie Jones Books (KJB) is to showcase writing that deserves attention, but that may not fit into "the present dollar-driven bottom line of mainstream publishing," Jones says. The author says the process of setting up its list "has been slow and extremely precise. We do not want a single book to not be as polished, as perfectly structured and executed, as it can possibly be."

Part of the KJB process is including its collective of volunteers in the acquisitions' decision-making process. The publishing team includes current and recent grad students, as well as invested members of the community, and their roles range from media relations to event planning to line editing. Every voice in the KJB collective has a say in the publishing process and that personal investment results in bound books the team can feel good about debuting for readers.

That's what it's really about. Volunteers with small presses and journals are driven with passion when it comes to seeing good writing in print. The frustration of recognizing talented authors but feeling helpless in not seeing these authors gain attention has been the catalyst behind a number of similar ventures.

In early 2011, Molly Gaudry, author of *We Take Me Apart*, announced on her social media platforms that she intended to start offering publicity services for small press authors as she felt there was a need to draw more attention to these authors. With an overwhelming response from her peers and the literary community, that goal quickly morphed into something with a much larger vision. Later that same year, Gaudry founded and began directing The Lit Pub, whose board of advisors includes Richard Nash, Mona Anita Olsen, and Jesse Bockstedt.

The Lit Pub is an independent publishing company that specializes in hybrid literature, crossing genres with experimental and traditional forms. In addition to publishing a select number of titles, the group also cross-promotes and collaborates with other small presses. Every day on The Lit Pub blog, it also shares reader recommendations for new and noteworthy books, literary magazines, and other relevant news, including author interviews.

This is but one example of how an invested author acted on what she perceived to be a void in the publishing world and took the chance on offering opportunities to other writers. A small kernel of an idea, a bit of editorial and publishing experience, and the support of peers and other editors can quickly turn a concept into a real, working model for promoting literature.

Finding a niche

Katerina Stoykova-Klemer, whose books include *The Porcupine of Mind*, had a vision in wanting to bring greater attention to poetry with a specific goal in mind. When she founded Accents Publishing, Stoykova-Klemer developed the mission to produce books with an affordable publication format. The result is that its chapbooks have a $5 price point.

The editor credits her personal experience as an author for teaching her valuable lessons in publishing. "Going through the process as an author helped me gather critical knowledge and helped me put myself into the shoes of the publishers," she says. Prior to starting Accents, Stoykova-Klemer worked with a number of high-tech companies that brought together her love of books and technology and gave her experience in creating books for electronic and print mediums.

Accents Publishing positioned itself to focus on quality, but with a mind to how readers buy books. "The decision to offer chapbooks at no more than $5 is very important to us, and paramount to our philosophy as a publisher," Stoykova-Klemer says. "We believe that people love to read. Moreover, people love buying books, giving books as gifts, and perhaps most importantly, supporting their author friends by buying their books. But the caveat is that people also want to feel good about their purchases. This is as true for a book as it is for a loaf of bread or a dishwasher."

Focusing on the combination of quality and efficiency, Stoykova-Klemer believes Accents Publishing offers as much to its authors as to its readers. "For our authors, this means that they won't have to wait a year or more before their work is published, and they will find it easier to sell their books, while at the same time feeling good about the value of the product that we are providing to their readers."

Zinta Astairs also had a focused goal in mind when she launched *The Smoking Poet*, an online literary journal. "I wanted to give a spotlight to writers and artists in my own neck of the woods—greater Kalamazoo, known for its high count of accomplished writers and artists, and Michigan in general." Astairs says the journal often uses college interns interested in creative writing and publishing to assist the magazine's editorial team. "These interns have been a joy to work with and, hopefully, they learn from the experience, too."

While the core focus of *The Smoking Poet* may be on regional work, the journal has editors based in and outside of Michigan and accepts work from writers far and wide. This has had an impact not only with regard to publication content, but for the editor's own personal development as well. "The networking born from all these years of publishing *TSP* has been extensive," Astairs says. "I can't even count all the wonderful connections I have made in my own community, but also far beyond it, even internationally."

Responding to regional need was also the determining factor for publisher Jeanetta Calhoun Mish. "Mongrel Empire Press was established in response to a need for another press that actively sought out and encouraged regional and vernacular writing," she says, adding that its focus is on writers who are active in the greater Oklahoma, Southern Missouri, and North Texas literary scenes. Six years later, the press has published more than 25 books, many of which have gone on to win national and state awards and recognition.

Money is not a bad word

It is a frequent misconception that launching a literary journal or small press will break the publisher's bank. Too, it is often considered that acts of literary citizenship should be exclusively of a volunteer basis—which will often result in expenses coming out of the do-gooder's pocket. This is not always, nor does it need to be, the case.

When author Kelly Davio teamed up with Joe Ponepinto, the two literary masterminds were determined to launch a print and online journal that not only paid writers for their contributions, but also brought in funds to help sustain the operation. The result is *Tahoma Literary Review*, which debuted in 2014.

"Compensating the writers we publish was as important in planning *TLR* as was publishing great literature," Ponepinto says. "We've both studied literary journal models for several years, and we've learned that although writers deserve to be paid for the time and effort it takes to produce a publishable poem or story, very few journals actually do so."

The duo's frustration at unpaid markets for writers was but one driving force of their mission. "If you put your ear to the ground in the literary world," Davio says, "you'll hear a steady hum of discontent about the fact that many writers aren't paid for their work, other than in exposure. You'll hear people upset about submission fees. You'll hear people repeating the phrase that 'money should flow to the writer.' I think we need to take those feelings seriously, but we also need to ask, 'okay, where's the money going to come from?'"

Charging submission fees to writers, particularly when presses use outside systems such as Submittable, is becoming a commonplace reality as publishers seek a way to sustain their operations. "Instead of hiding from that fact or pretending that there's some enormous, untapped readership waiting to be found," Davio says, "we wanted to see what would happen if we put forth a model in which the literary world could support itself both artistically *and* financially."

Their solution was to utilize those submission fees to pay professional rates to writers published in *Tahoma Literary Review*. When submitters see that their modest submission fee has a direct impact on paying writers, it's easier to digest, says Ponepinto. "We came up with the idea of using submission fees, and eventually grants, print sales and donations, to create a pool from which writers could be paid," he adds. "We studied a variety of journals and queried many writers to determine where to set our fees, and coupled advancements in digital publishing with our personal business and graphic design experience to reduce production and distribution costs. Because our fees are slightly higher than other journals, we also wanted to make sure that every submitter, published or not, received some value for their payment, so we created a password protected section of interviews and craft advice available only to submitters and supporters."

Tahoma Literary Review required little upfront costs to prepare for launch. Outside of its Web site start-up costs and some introductory advertising, Ponepinto says its personal commitment is more related to time: for reading and editing, designing the issues, and marketing.

While Ponepinto says "when you do what you love, it hardly seems like work," the editorial team has ensured that their enterprise should see financial gain. "As publishers we have built in a small percentage of the income as payment for ourselves, which we believe is fair compensation for our efforts and experience. Some of what we pay ourselves goes back into building the journal's image and helping publicize our writers."

A common explanation for the demise of volunteer-run journals is that those in charge simply cannot absorb the costs any longer than they already have. Depending on the size and frequency of publication, production costs and time commitments can go from manageable to burdensome in a matter of months. "When we first began to talk about the possibility of *TLR*, sustainability was an important part of our conversations," says Davio. "We wanted to be sure not to bite off more than we could chew in terms of workload, and we didn't want to have such high projections for our financial success that we couldn't deliver on our promises to writers—we see ourselves as entering a marathon rather than a sprint."

Davio adds that editorial burnout is "a real danger in these kinds of enterprises, and so we have found ways to reduce the amount of time we spend on the tasks we don't like so that we can focus on the aspects of editing that are gratifying and that feed our enthusiasm for the work."

Paying writers for their pieces adds merit to the publication process, Ponepinto says, and likewise validates the journal as a professional operation. "Every time we pay a writer for something she's written, it encourages her and others to keep writing, keep creating." Davio adds that their model also pushes back "against the devaluation of literary writing. We're living in a moment when a novel can sell for 99 cents on Amazon, and when you consider the time, labor, and talent that go into writing a book-length work, 99 cents is a startling comment on what our culture values. We think literature is worth something, and we think it's possible for the literary world to work collaboratively to reverse that kind of cultural depreciation."

Money can sometimes seem like a dirty word in publishing. Writers infrequently talk about their income in a public forum. Royalties and freelance payments seem to operate on a hushed level. This can be frustrating to published and unpublished writers alike as most writers hope to be somehow compensated for their published work.

Sharing the ins and outs of the publishing industry, along with concrete financial discussions, informs the broader community about realities and expectations. Knowledge is power and sharing that knowledge helps create a more informed, more powerful writing community.

When industry expert Jane Friedman, former publisher of *Writer's Digest*, set out to launch the digital magazine *Scratch Magazine*, she was intent on breaking the financial discussion barrier. "I've always been interested how, why, and when writers get educated on the business side of their craft—especially when so many schools deliberately keep discussions of money out of the classroom," says Friedman. "I'm also an advocate for industry transparency, and writers having access to the information they need to make informed decisions about their careers. With so much change and upheaval across the publishing industry, this transparency is becoming more important than ever."

Scratch offers a two-part model for reader access. Quarterly digital issues are available by subscription, but readers have free access to online articles, resources, and the popular Who Pays Writers database—a crowd-sourced listing of freelance pay rates. "Who Pays Writers was started in December 2012 by my business partner on *Scratch*, Manjula Martin. She launched it partly as a result of a Twitter conversation about how useful it would be if writers openly shared information about pay rates," says Friedman.

While money may be a taboo subject for many writers, helping writers gain access to industry standards is a valuable service—and it is certainly an act of literary citizenship to educate one another on how to sustain a writing life. "In the sense that we're trying to serve, inform, and educate writers about the publishing community—and bring attention to a diversity of people, perspectives, and trends therein—I think so," Friedman says. "We envision developing a community of writers for whom it's no longer taboo to talk about money and business, or how one makes a sustainable living through their art."

As Friedman, Davio, and Ponepinto suggest, money doesn't have to be a four-letter word. Financial burden is often a real factor in whether a would-be literary citizen embarks on launching a journal or small press, and writers certainly hope to receive fair payment for their published work. By working together and addressing financial matters in an honest manner, these authors and editors are paving the way for more open discussions of funding the arts. In bridging the gap between costs and benefits for our literary projects, collaborative efforts can ensure successful sustainable models, financially and otherwise.

Collaborative efforts

As evidenced with the Kaylie Jones Books business model, a growing trend in small press publishing is to open up the editorial process to include a number of invested readers with similar passions. In a similar vein, Booktrope Publishing makes its business model transparent to authors and readers alike by sharing its operational and financial structure on its Web site. Each book the publisher contracts has a dedicated team that works with the author from initial submission acceptance to post-publication marketing. The author, proofreader, editor, designer, and publicity manager each receive a specific percentage of the book's revenues. This may, in reality, be not unlike mainstream publishing, but Booktrope makes its finances transparent to others to take away the guessing game of how revenues are divided in this team-based model.

"Booktrope was founded on an idea of teamwork, and with a conscious choice to create a system that was fair and open," says cofounder and editor Katherine Sears. "No one on a publishing team in our system can succeed at the expense of another, so in many ways, they must act as a cohesive community."

Literary citizens interested in starting a small press may examine how other entrepreneurial minds took an idea through to reality with success. As these authors have demonstrated, great concepts are most often successfully executed through collaborative teamwork.

Betsy Teter, director of Hub City, explains how the nonprofit writing center, bookshop, and press grew out of a shared passion among friends. "We, the founders, had met each other in a coffee shop back in 1995. In fact, it was the first real coffee shop to open in Spartanburg, founded by a guy from California who just happened through town a year earlier. From our own experience, we knew that comfortable and cool public spaces were key to community energy. Just having places where people could meet each other could spark a change in the course of a community," she says. "We proposed to the city that we help them open an alternative arts space and artist residency program in a run-down end of downtown."

From the beginning, the organizers of Hub City were focused on making Spartanburg a more livable community by enhancing the local arts scene and preserving as much of the area history as possible. The group restored a downtown property and hired on a few staff members, but it continues to make regular use of volunteers from the community.

"I think our volunteers see themselves as being part of something larger than just a two hour shift at the cash register, or proofing a manuscript, or making coffee at a writing conference. They see themselves as part of a community of writers and readers. They also get access to events and writers they might not otherwise," Teter says. "We have so many broad opportunities for volunteering that if people don't like one assignment, they can try something else. Right now we have a waiting line for people who want to volunteer in the bookshop."

Keeping it professional

While these authors show the possibilities in starting a small press, Kaylie Jones offers a few tips in ensuring success at every level. She says her research uncovered a number of presses that didn't pay as much attention to professional editing, resulting in books laden with typos and sloppy sentences. "This is something to really pay attention to," she says. "Most people want to rush into this arena, because it is in fact very easy to set up an e-book publishing company, but very few have the experience, knowledge, and resources to really stand out as professional enterprises."

Jones suggests that potential publishers find a solid team to share the workload, establish priorities, and ensure professionalism is always at the forefront of the press. "Open Road Media is a great success because they have at their helm Jane Friedman, the former head of HarperCollins. She has brought an incredible team aboard, and the site, the works, and the public relations departments are exceptional," Jones says. "I would urge potential publishers to do their research, and to spend their time and energy on the quality of the works themselves, rather than the smoke and mirrors."

Writers and readers who want to take action, who wish to contribute to contemporary publishing and promote new literature, may find starting an online literary journal to be a relatively feasible idea. Yet, as Jones noted, even with the ease of publishing content online, editors carry a responsibility in publishing quality work and presenting their material in a professional, engaging manner.

Georgia Ann Banks-Martin took over as editor and publisher of *New Mirage Journal* in 2010, when Jerome Brooks stepped down and passed on the reins to her. One of the first things Banks-Martin did as editor was change the Web host and platform for the journal. She says the original site was "difficult to manage due to technical concerns, cost, and limited template options." The editor researched other viable options for both quality of design and cost efficiency and found that moving the journal to a free platform was the best option.

The user-friendly platform has not only saved the journal overhead costs, but also attracted a larger readership. "Wordpress offers more flexibility and allows readers greater access. Readers can now interact with the writers and choose to follow the journal so they are alerted when there is something new to read," she says, adding that *New Mirage Journal* now has as many as 3,000 visitors in a day, compared with the few hundred it had before.

The editor suggests that would-be publishers consider every opportunity to cut costs. "Make use of tools that are free. This includes sending submission information to the Creative Writers Opportunities List on Yahoo, creating a *Poets & Writers* listing, and using free artwork," she says, noting that *New Mirage Journal* uses free clipart for its logo banner.

"If the basics can be obtained free, there is little to no cost to start your journal," Banks-Martin says. "If you are interested in copywriting, having your own domain name, a custom webpage and hosting, Council of Literary Magazines and Presses membership, and sound clips you will have to pay for those services. All of this can be overwhelming, but the stress is worth your time because you are helping others. It is the existence of small presses and magazines that help writers the world over to develop name recognition, readerships, and careers."

Would-be publishers should consider not only the potential costs for launching and maintaining a journal or press, but also the personal time investment that is necessary for running a professional operation. *Hippocampus Magazine*'s Donna Talarico says the "feel-good aspect" outweighs the time and effort required to managing a journal, while her dedicated volunteer team ensures that each issue is produced with attention to quality. "I have a marketing and PR background, so my biggest caution is this," she says. "Cheap or free templates give people the illusion that *starting* an online literary magazine is easy. I think it is the sustainability that some people don't think about."

The management of a quality literary journal includes more than posting a few submissions online, and Talarico says a publication's long-term viability requires forethought. "What is your strategy, what are your long-term plans? Most of what happens in a literary magazine happens offline, behind the scenes. I've seen a few pop up and then drop off the face of the Earth within months. It's a lot of work," she says, "and I think there is always room for a good magazine, but I sometimes fear that the ease of creating websites gives the false impression that running a magazine is a breeze. I've set milestones for *Hippocampus*, and even though we're only a few years old, we're still brand new and there is a lot more to come!"

It may indeed seem possible to come up with an idea for an online magazine and launch it within the same weekend, but experienced editors urge careful study of the market before making a debut. "Running a successful literary endeavor in today's economic environment is a blend of artistic and real-world skills," says *TLR*'s Joe Ponepinto. "You can't ignore either aspect and expect to be around for very long. Study your art extensively—read the best work out there. Study craft like crazy—develop your personal style as an editor and writer. From the business end, research the market to see what readers and writers expect, and to determine where opportunities for innovation lie."

TLR copublisher Kelly Davio emphasizes the significant learning experience one can receive in apprenticing with an already established publication. "There's quite a bit more complexity on the business end of editing that I could have imagined when I first started out, and I'm glad I worked alongside experienced editors rather than founding a journal only to fold immediately," she says. "Once you know the possibilities and the pitfalls of the business, it's a little easier to find a sustainable business model for the long term."

Starting small and setting attainable goals may be one way to get a new journal off the ground. Likewise, focusing on a specific audience may help focus a publication and ensure room for growth—which may come sooner than anticipated. *The Rusty Toque* grew out of the University of Western Ontario when Kathryn Mockler had a vision to showcase emerging writers.

"It was a student journal for the first issue, and then my co-editor, Aaron Schneider, and I made the leap and opened up submissions to all writers." The online journal now includes multiple genres of writing, Canadian and international book reviews, as well as art in all formats, including video and sound.

The journal continues to be run on a volunteer basis. "In order to run a journal you have to genuinely be interested in other writers and artists. Right now I'm enjoying it so it doesn't feel like work to me," Mockler says, adding that "the first couple of years are the hardest. My co-editor and I have slowly brought people on to help us. We now have a film editor and an art editor, and we're working with community and student volunteers, but getting this in order takes time and getting people invested takes time. However, bringing on too many people too soon can affect the vision of your journal."

And, while the perks of managing a literary journal include greater exposure to new work and the pride of publishing new voices, Mockler says there are less than thrilling aspects of publishing that are equally good learning experiences. "The downside of running a journal is rejecting people. There isn't enough money to pay all the people we would like to publish and there isn't enough time to interview all the writers we would like to interview. There are many factors that come into play when making editorial decisions," she says. "Just because a work gets rejected doesn't mean we hate it or that the person who submitted is a bad writer. It often means that it wasn't a fit for that issue."

Determining need

While it's certainly rewarding to offer valuable opportunities to fellow writers, the relative ease of publishing online should not be the main reason an author launches a new publication. As Georgia Ann Banks-Martin and Donna Talarico point out, it's the long-term maintenance that can burden a publisher. Running a journal can exhaust one's time, energy, creativity, and personal savings account.

Jessie Carty, editor of *Referential Magazine*, also suggests that potential publishers consider the true purpose of adding to an already large pool of established journals. "When people ask me about starting an online magazine I first ask them, why? If you have a particular type of project or audience that you feel is under-served then go for it," she says. "If you just want to have a literary magazine, and it is just like all the others, then why?"

Referential Magazine stands out from the norm as it asks contributors to respond and refer to specific past works, furthering the connection and conversation of one writer's piece to the next. And, like Banks-Martin, Carty has been able to balance the demands of running a journal. "I've been able to keep expenses pretty low, but that also keeps me from paying writers. I also think having a specific type of journal has helped limit our submissions, which has kept me mostly sane," she says. "It is definitely something I find fulfilling, though. I love publishing amazing writing, and I have had the chance to work with a variety of editors over the years as well. Finding a community of writers, readers, and editors who can join together in a conversation is at the heart of what I want to do as a writer and reader."

While there are limitless opportunities for starting a new small press or journal, interested literary citizens might find just as much satisfaction in lending a hand to an already established publisher. As many of these editors have stated, volunteers are at a premium and can offer just as much to the publisher as volunteers can gain from their involvement. In addition to contributing to the publication's mission, a volunteer will learn firsthand editorial or marketing experience, add practical skills to his or her resume, discover new voices in contemporary literature, and widen his or her social and peer network to help stave off those more solitary moments of being a writer.

Whether supporting a press or journal directly, or in assisting a select number of authors through alternate avenues, there are countless ways to participate in celebrating new literature. In the next chapter, we'll look at a few more ways literary citizens like yourself have created opportunities for others through innovative means.

8

Community Outreach

There are ample opportunities for adding literary acts of kindness to our routine. Encouraging fellow writers, sharing recommendations with others, reviewing books, and volunteering at community events are some of the easiest avenues to commit to literary citizenship. Later in this chapter, we'll look at a few writers who have taken their love of literature to the street level, coming up with innovative ways to reach new audiences while showcasing their creative flair.

Yet, engaging with the community need not be restricted to grassroots efforts alone. A number of literary citizens, not unlike you or me, took the seed of an idea, formulated a plan, and gathered the support of like-minded collaborators to form a larger platform. If you're looking to make an impact with an established group within a broader community, you might consider offering your skills and time to a group that not only promotes literature, but also meets challenges with literacy or other social concerns.

National opportunities

While I unfortunately can't fit in every opportunity worthy of a mention, this small sampling of groups demonstrates the breadth of organizations that rely on community involvement. They range from those focused on mentoring at-risk youth or troubled adults, providing opportunities for underserved or underrepresented writers, offering literacy services, and more.

VIDA: Women in Literary Arts was founded in 2009 to "explore critical and cultural perceptions of writing by women."[1] The organization includes members from around the country who share the goal of promoting writing by women to the community at large. While VIDA may be most known for "the count"—a system that measures the regularity, and irregularity, of women being published and critiqued in the larger community— the organization also hosts events and encourages community discourse. It also offers an online community of writers, Her Kind, to connect members and general readers alike.

"I started volunteering early on," says Amy King, the Communications Liaison & Interview Correspondent for VIDA. "Cate Marvin invited me after she saw me posting on my blog about publishing disparities. It has been incredibly rewarding to find people aware of the nuances and complexities of the literary publishing world."

King says conversations stemming from the VIDA community have opened up widespread discussion about women

---

[1] VIDA: Women in Literary Arts, vidaweb.org.

in publishing and related issues. "The interest in this conversation deepens each month, and the contributions from readers, writers, editors and publishers continue to inform where we might head and what we might look at and discuss next," she says. "The literary world is even larger than I imagined, simply based on the enormous web reaching around the globe. As well, the enthusiasm and support for our endeavors are only equaled by people's hopes that a unified but diverse group of like-minded individuals might actually have an equalizing impact on the literary landscape."

With a similar mission in mind, Canadian poet and essayist Gillian Jerome founded CWILA: Canadian Women in the Literary Arts. The organization unites those with a common vision of feminist values to advocate "the importance of strong and active female perspectives and presences within the Canadian literary landscape."[2] In its first year of operations, the organization documented and analyzed more than 2,500 book reviews from Canadian newspapers and literary journals.

Included in CWILA's programming is a public awareness campaign focused on issues related to gender, race, and sexuality within Canadian literature, a Critic-in-Residence program that selects one writer annually to collaborate with the greater reviews community, and a national critical culture conference. The organization encourages members and the general public to get involved in supporting its mission. To aid this effort, the CWILA Web site makes available a resource list of Canadian publications

---

[2]Canadian Women in the Literary Arts, cwila.com.

that publish literary reviews and criticism, as well as an interview series with review publication editors.

Inclusivity begins early and we all want our youth to grow into creative and skilled adults. As such, a number of organizations are focused on offering assistance to young writers. 826 National is a nonprofit organization with eight regional writing and tutoring centers across the country. In its focus on providing opportunities to underresourced students aged 6–18, the organization encourages young writers to explore their creativity and improve their writing skills, while also providing resources to teachers to invigorate their writing classes. Volunteers and interns have options to assist in event planning, program evaluation, fundraising, administration, and marketing. There are opportunities to assist at both the national and regional levels. For those interested in contributing to an organization that combines creative and practical writing, 826 National has this to say on its Web site:

> Our mission is based on the understanding that great leaps in learning can happen with one-on-one attention, and that strong writing skills are fundamental to future success.
>
> —826national.org

Similarly, Girls Write Now, housed in New York City, is a nationally recognized organization focused on providing educational support and creative opportunities for at-risk and underserved girls and young women. Its activities include mentorships, workshops, guest author talks, and performance and publication opportunities. The organization was founded in 1998 and until 2005, Girls Write Now operated on an entirely volunteer basis.

"In a world where it is increasingly hard for people without connections or resources to make their voices heard," says Kamy Wicoff, chair of the board of directors, "an organization like Girls Write Now, which empowers high-need, at-risk girls to tell their stories and author change in their lives, is critical to creating the kind of world I want to live in and the kind of literature I want to read."

Wicoff spends her time helping with fundraising efforts and engaging publishing companies and literary agencies in supporting the next generation of women writers. Volunteers from the community are utilized in areas such as marketing, fundraising, program development, and mentorship. "The mentors, all professional women writers, dive deep with their mentees, meeting intensively every week and attending monthly craft workshops, where mentors and mentees write alongside each other," says Wicoff. "The incredible thing is that we have a waiting list for mentors. We had to turn almost 80% of our [mentor] applicants away this year. To me, it's a testament to writers' deep need for community, which they find at Girls Write Now not just with the girls but with their fellow mentors and peers."

At the heart of the organization is making the connection between creativity, writing, and lifelong success strategies. In essence, the community at Girls Write Now is fostering future literary citizens, as evidenced on its Web site:

> Writing passionately is many things: an act of power, an act of courage, an act of generosity. Every member of our community shares a passion for mastering our craft and a deep conviction

that our work has the power to enrich the lives of others as well as our own.

—GirlsWriteNow.org

Freelance publicity consultant Lauren Cerand, a previous board member of Girls Write Now and continuing supporter, currently offers her time and expertise to PEN Center USA, which works on multiple levels: to protect the rights and freedoms of writers around the world, to promote interest in literature, and to foster a diverse literary community. Volunteers may be engaged with mentorship projects, public literary events, and international human rights campaigns. In particular, PEN advocates on behalf of imprisoned writers and those who face "political prosecution, persecution, and censorship."[3]

"It's been fantastic," Cerand says of her involvement with PEN, adding that she cohosted "the launch party for their World Voices Festival and newly-revamped website, an event to which hundreds of people attended."

While national organizations often offer opportunities both across the country and within select regions, you're bound to find nonprofits similar to these in your own backyard. As an example, InsideOut Literary Arts Project is a nationally recognized organization that operates on a local level in Metro Detroit. Poet Terry Blackhawk, whose books include *Escape Artist*, is the founder and director of this arts education community dedicated to

---

[3]Pen Center USA, penusa.org.

at-risk youth. InsideOut runs a poets-in-schools program that serves more than 5,000 youths annually. With a focus on poetry, the organization helps students develop their self-expression and creativity, while giving them opportunities to perform their work in front of audiences.

InsideOut volunteers are always welcome, and the organization also relies on committed literary citizens willing to serve in the Writer-In-Residence program. Internships are also available within specific areas such as grant writing. Those interested in offering their time and talent to developing young writers may find their mission statement helpful:

> By immersing students in the joy and power of poetry and literary self-expression, InsideOut inspires them to think broadly, create bravely and share their voices with the wider world. Guided by professional writers and celebrated by publications and performances, youth learn that their stories and ideas matter and that their pens can launch them off the page into extraordinary lives.
>
> —InsideOutDetroit.org

Act locally

Even volunteers with larger organizations may find unique ways to offer their time and skills to the local community. The following inspiring activities may prompt you to consider what you can offer in your own neighborhood.

Poet Joy Gaines-Friedler, author of *Dutiful Heart*, mentors Detroit Public School children as part of her work with Inside-Out Literary Arts Project, but she also works with two more local projects in an effort to encourage creativity and self-expression through writing. "I bring creative writing to troubled young adults, many of whom have had to deal with issues of suicidal tendencies, gender identity, drug abuse, bullying, and other kinds of traumas," the author says of her work with Community Network Services. "I have also had the honor of working at Common Ground with family members and parents of murdered children."

Gaines-Friedler says she hopes her writing students find a way to look outward and observe the world and to write without the fear of being judged. "Spelling doesn't matter, nor does grammar. This time is meant for creativity," she says. "I tell them my story. I tell them how I survived the loss of my two best friends—one was murdered, the other died from AIDS—and how I grew up in a troubled home that required me to leave as soon as I could. When I began writing, many years later, I began to celebrate and honor my life, trauma and all."

Exposing community members to the joys of creative expression is the driving force behind many of these organizations. Christina Springer, an artist who combines her passion for poetry, text art, and dance, offered free "Living the Writing Life" workshops to the Pittsburgh community. Springer is a fellow with Cave Canem, a foundation created by poets Toi Derricotte and Cornelius Eady to bring greater representation and opportunity for African-American poets. Through her involvement with

Cave Canem and with the support of the Pittsburgh Foundation, Springer applied the mission of the national organization and offered opportunities on a more local level.

Ife-Chudeni Oputa, another Cave Canem fellow, says the organization opens its doors to writers in and outside of the summer retreats. "Approximately fifteen first-year fellows are accepted for the retreat every year, but there are a lot of other ways to get involved in the organization, especially if you're in the New York area—for example, writing workshops, readings, and Poets on Craft panels," she says. "Workshops have also been conducted in Pittsburgh, and fellows around the country often curate regional events," Oputa adds, in cities such as Baltimore and St Louis.

Providing community access without barriers is ideal for creating an inviting arena for those who cannot spend limited funds on artistic engagement. Writers associated with New York State Writers Institute regularly offer Community Writers Workshops that are free and accessible to the general public. Rebecca Wolff, a fellow with the institute, recently offered an 8-week poetry workshop in Hudson, New York, and Writer-in-Residence Jo Page has offered a 7-week short prose workshop.

Yet, a literary citizen need not belong to a major organization to develop community events such as these. After all, not every region has convenient access to a large network of supporters and peers. When poet and editor Neil Shepard accepted a job in Johnson VT, he wondered what opportunities for community engagement existed in such a small town. "Of course, there were a few writing colleagues at the college, and I knew other writers around the state," he says, "but Vermont roads are narrow and winding, and especially during the long winter months, we travel less here, our associations reduced to email."

As the founding editor of *Green Mountains Review*, Shepard had a built-in community, but he longed for a larger "flesh and bone" network of peers. To achieve that goal, Shepard directed the Green Mountains Writers Workshop, a 2-week summer workshop that was successful, but still left the writer wanting more for his local area. "Finally in 1988, I met the president and founder of the Vermont Studio Center, Jon Gregg, and began an association with this Johnson-based colony for visual artists," says Shepard. "By 1990, I had convinced him to add writers to the mix."

This outreach led to Shepard directing the writers program at the Vermont Studio that welcomed emerging, mid-career, and well-established writers. "For me, as a writer, it intensified my education with weekly craft talks and readings by some of the best writers in America," says Shepard. "The VSC brought to my life daily literary conversations in the dining hall, at the local coffee shop and bookstore, along the sidewalks of the town. And it infused our small town of Johnson with new energy and vitality. Not only did the VSC invite writers and artists from all fifty American states, but it also developed grants and attracted writers and artists from abroad—from Asia, Africa, Europe, Central and South America—and so the lily-white town of Johnson was suddenly infused with new cultures, complexities and challenges, as well as with new demands for goods and services and an influx of new money into its economy."

Venues including libraries, community centers, senior centers, and other common grounds most often welcome proposals to lead residencies, informal talks, workshops, mentoring sessions, and open mics. Author Monique Antonette Lewis developed At The Inkwell, which offers both a reading series and an online resource for writers. Lewis says she started the program to share her passion for writing with others. She approached KGB, a famed New York city bar and literary hub, and proposed her idea for a reading series. While Lewis says she had to convince the owner to take a chance on her—someone he didn't know well among a sea of writers and organizers he was accustomed to working with—she worked tirelessly to promote the first event of many, and the series launched with great success.

"Nearly every seat was full at the first reading," Lewis says. Thanks to her preevent marketing efforts, the owner was interested in seeing the series continue, as she "had built up a positive credibility." Now, the reading series features authors from within and outside of New York, and Lewis often shares calls for readers on her Facebook page to offer opportunities to writers traveling through the area.

Accompanying the reading series, Lewis also shares writing resources, book reviews, and author interviews on the Web site attheinkwell.com. Everything shared on the Web site is offered free to interested readers. "I want to give authors of all genres an opportunity to promote their books through book reviews, especially those who are self-published," she says. "These authors are promoting their work solely on their own and they need every bit of help they can get in an increasingly competitive market."

Lewis adds that her intent on sharing the personal stories of writers can offer inspiration to emerging and established writers alike. "I think the features can give another perspective on who the authors are and not just their writing. People love to connect to the authors and find out how they came up with the stories they wrote."

Poetic visibility

As part of National Poetry Month, a few community members in London, Ontario, brought public attention to late poet Colleen Thibaudeau. The Canadian poet, recognized for her substantial volunteer work supporting writers across Canada, inspired the local community to share her poem "Balloon" on a billboard neighboring a busy downtown intersection. Kitty McKay Lewis, general manager of the Canadian press Brick Books, says the project was "spearheaded by poet Christine Walde and funded by Poetry London, Brick Books, and London Public Library. Colleen knew about it before she passed away but the billboard went up in April after her passing," she says. "We had a fun launch with balloons and lemonade."

Poet Tammy Gomez also enjoys finding unique ways to share poetry with the public. She brought members of her community together to create a poem the length of a city block—*on* a city block—and this is but one of her public poetry projects. The Mexican-American Texas-born writer says she works to "engage the audience in an experience with poetry that falls outside of the mainstream. Ultimately, my interactive, performed, published, and produced work seeks to create bridges between peoples."

The block poem project took 5 years from conception to reality. The work aimed "to bring community together in a cooperative, non-proprietary, and creative experience in public space wherein folks—children as well as adults—help build a poem about being a good neighbor on your block," Gomez says, adding that they used "recycled and repurposed wooden 2x4 blocks placed end to end to form a city block-long poem." The poet says passersby wanting to see the whole context of the poem had to "walk from one end to the next in order to read it in its entirety."

Todd Boss, a poet from Minnesota, also hopes to have found a way to bring poetry to a larger audience. As the cofounder of Motionpoems, a nonprofit film organization, he creates short films inspired by contemporary poems. These films are shared at festivals, cinemas, museums, libraries, and schools. To maximize audience exposure, Motionpoems makes films available online for free viewing. "Audience reaction has been overwhelmingly positive," Boss says, "but that's because we're hearing from enthusiasts. Motionpoems is still too small to boast a broad viewing audience of non-poetry readers, so it's hard to evaluate our impact there."

Boss says he and his collaborator, Angella Kassube, were motivated by their enjoyment of poetry and their desire to share the language of poetry in a more familiar medium. "Poets, for their part, are ecstatic about the project, primarily for two reasons," he says. "It helps them tell their poems in a new way and to a new audience, and it recognizes poets as artists worthy of celebration and lavish artistic attention. Poets too rarely consider that poems aren't endpoints but potential starting-points for other artists."

Merging his love of poetry and motion pictures was a natural fit. "Film still speaks some of the primal languages that are responsible for poetry's storytelling origins as an oral and performing art, whereas much of contemporary poetry has forgotten those roots," Boss says. "Meanwhile, we're hearing from readers and students who discover us online, and tell us that viewing our films has inspired more than one book purchase. That's what it's about for us—sampling poetry to would-be readers."

Online and on the air

Considering literature's history with oral tradition, it's no wonder a number of writers are sharing their love of creative writing across the air waves. TuneIn.com offers links to radio shows across the country that focus on books and authors, while National Public Radio often features author interviews and discussions.

Quiddity is a monthly program on Illinois Public Radio, as well as being distributed through the Public Radio Exchange, which is hosted in conjunction with the international print literary journal published by Benedictine University. Managing editor Jim Warner says *Quiddity* provides "the voice behind the page" with interviews and performances that enrich the overall experience with the magazine. "Our radio show also exposes our journal to an audience who may not be familiar with us in print, but as a fan of public radio, appreciates the arts," he says.

"*Quiddity* allows us to go beyond work and present thoughtful and engaging conversation, giving the listeners a chance to be a part of the discussion, and another point of entry into the work," Warner says. "I think the most successful literary endeavors are the ones which seek to not only build bridges within arts communities but beyond the traditional audiences as well. Art is only as good as the conversation it inspires, and *Quiddity* hopes to provide a thoughtful and engaging space for that conversation to happen."

To broaden the audience for poetry, Sandee Gertz Umbach, author of *The Pattern Maker's Daughter*, joined forces with a local popular radio station. "We do a lot at the non-profit art center we founded here to bring poetry into the public domain," she says. "For National Poetry Month, we had different residents of the community read their favorite poem, or a suggested poem, on the air during 'Prime Drive Time' mornings and then had them discuss it with the DJ on-air. People reading the poems were everyone from judges and elected officials to teachers and moms and dads known in the community."

While the radio station was known more for its oldies programming than for poetry, the author says the producers were happy to take a risk. "It was very different than anything they would normally do! In the end, they said that they received good feedback from listeners and that it was all positive." Community participation continued off the air, too, as local partnering coffeehouses and libraries offered discussions of the poems featured on the station each day.

Adding to the airwaves is Katerina Stoykova-Klemer, the founder of Accents Publishing, who also hosts a weekly radio show on WRFL 88.1FM in Lexington, Kentucky. *Accents: A Radio Show for Literature, Art, and Culture* features writers and literary citizens from around the world. Her mission is to promote local, national, and international arts alike, and the topics include new book discussions, author interviews, and calls for submissions from literary publications. To broaden public interaction, the poet invites listeners to send in their own writing to be shared on the air. On her Web site,[4] Stoykova-Klemer archives past radio shows as MP3 recordings, making the broadcasts accessible anytime, anywhere.

With a specific focus on helping writers of all genres find homes for their work, author Allison Joseph began CCWWRP: The Creative Writing Opportunities Listserv offered for free on Yahoo. Joseph is the author of six collections of poetry, the editor of *Crab Orchard Review*, and an associate professor in the writing program at Southern Illinois University-Carbondale. In recognition of her various efforts in volunteering and mentoring emerging writers, Joseph was awarded the 2012 George Garrett Award for Outstanding Community Service in Literature, which is administered by the Association of Writers & Writing Programs.

Online venues are certainly a great way to connect with writers across the world. It was with this in mind that Kamy Wicoff

---

[4]Accents Radio Archives, http://katerinaklemer.com/radio.html.

developed SheWrites.com, an online forum for women writers. The community discussion site has grown to tens of thousands of active members from across the nation and from more than 30 other countries. With a mission to empower women to use social media tools for community building and collaboration, the organization has also added an educational branch and an independent press to its program offerings.

"Founding She Writes with Deborah Siegel was one of the best things I ever did, and I would definitely do it again," says Wicoff. "Our vision, from the beginning, was to take the knowledge and expertise individual writers were acquiring in a rapidly changing publishing landscape—so rapidly changing it was nearly impossible to keep up—and share it in a transparent, supportive way that would benefit every member of the community." Their intent was to help writers avoid "reinventing the wheel every time she had to learn a new skill" like social media best practices, Web site design, and community event planning. In doing so, Wicoff says, "She Writes would enable that author to learn from others, saving invaluable time and energy, as long as she was also willing, when she had knowledge to share, to teach."

Wicoff says the idea for She Writes stemmed from a live and in-person salon of women writers she had been hosting for years in New York, along with memoirist and critic Nancy K. Miller. Their intent was to host a digital version of the salon, but they found that the desire for such an online community extended far beyond their immediate city. "There was a hunger for connection with other women writers of every genre, generation and skill level," Wicoff says, "and an intuitive grasp, from the beginning, of

Debbie's and my vision that participants at She Writes would be rewarded for generosity—with their knowledge, their expertise, and their support—above all else. A tone was set from day one that carries on to this day, and I think it is this warmth and openness that makes it such a valuable resource. It is a safe place, and it is also a high-quality, curated, intelligent place, and that makes it very powerful and appealing."

Close-knit communities

The beauty of literary citizenship is that writers and readers need not take grand leaps to make an impact in their community. Every one of us has something to offer to others and each region has a community awaiting support and celebration.

Lillian-Yvonne Bertram, author of *But A Storm is Blowing From Paradise*, has been a Bread Loaf Writers' Conference scholarship winner, a Cave Canem fellow, and a writer-in-residence at the Montana Artists' Refuge. In her experience, "offering workshops and readings or writing groups at places like senior centers has been awesome." In her effort to reach undeserved communities, Bertram put together a tour that offered workshops and readings at library branches and independent bookstores throughout northern California, focusing on areas "that didn't normally see reading tour traffic."

One of her recent projects involved a small group of peers who met in their undergraduate program and have maintained contact. "We have all benefited from good literary citizenship on the behalf of others, and now we are in a position and have the energies, enthusiasm, and hopefully the resources, to return the favor," the poet says. At the time of this writing, the group is planning a tour of "readings and free poetry and literary arts workshops at libraries and community spaces around the country," Bertram says. "The goal of the tour is not just to present our own work, but also to engage in lively and productive ways with the vast network of poets and writers that perhaps go unacknowledged by the mainstream poetry and literature world because they are not considered legitimate in the eyes of the academy."

Bertram says the group will include guerilla performances of People Against Poetry, an interactive performance pioneered by Adam Atkinson and S. E. Smith, in which "unsuspecting participants find themselves advocating passionately for the importance of keeping poetry and literary arts programs in public schools." The tour will be documented by Ben Pelhan, a poet and a filmmaker, along with volunteer camera operators, and Bertram says the events "will be produced as a documentary capturing the ways and places in which poetry is very much alive in these United States."

Closer to home, West Virginia writer Diane Tarantini supports others in her community by participating in a monthly reading series known as Morgantown Poets. "At each meeting, we host a featured writer. This person reads, offers craft and publishing counsel, and/or fields questions for about an hour," she says. "After that, we have an hour–long open mic session which features a variety of spoken word performances including poetry, prose, recitation, essay, and songs." Tarantini says these community events offer support to first-time readers, while also showcasing experienced local talents. In addition to the performance component, Tarantini enjoys the camaraderie of her peers, saying that she has found a home where she feels support and encouragement. "I like when we share submission opportunities," she says. "I also like when folks tell of their successes, and failures, so we can celebrate or commiserate together."

Jersey Shore Writers is a similar community group made up of just over a dozen participants. Hosted at the Jersey Shore Arts Center, a multiarts venue, the writing group meets with the simple goal of "publishing our work and staying alive as active writers," says member Patricia Florio. "We critique, read aloud, laugh, and discern what's going on in the publishing world, enter our work into literary contests, etc. In essence, we help one another, we enjoy one another's company, and we share our active writing projects in process."

The group opens its doors to the community with a reading series where authors from the tristate area visit and perform, and offer encouragement to aspiring writers. "It gives the residents of our Jersey Shore towns an opportunity to share in our art and the art of other writers," Florio says. "Our commonality in reading, listening, critiquing, and participating in one another's projects for the good of the community focuses us on projects that we want to accomplish individually and as a group."

South Carolina author Susan Tekulve agrees that the mere act of connecting with a few local and like-minded peers is one of the most rewarding activities of literary citizenship. "If you write regularly, you tend to spend large spaces of time alone, in your own head, so another central aspect of literary citizenship is finding those people who are actively and seriously engaged in the act of writing," she says. "My idea of literary citizenship hasn't changed much over the years. I usually have a couple of writing partners. These are usually other writers who are at about the same point in their careers as I am, with whom I can exchange work and share observations about books and writing. My writing partners and I respect each other, and we reciprocate by always making sure that we are reading each other's work attentively and with our highest level of expertise."

Regardless of group size, author Wayne Ude agrees that peer support is vital to the local and broader communities. "As a member of a critique group or a writers' association, you're an active member of the community. In a good critique group, everyone grows," he says. Yet, Ude offers advice to those working within a critique workshop. As important as it is to identify potential problems in another's work, he says, "it's equally important to point out strengths. Many writers, especially early in their careers, aren't aware of their strengths, and a critique group which focuses entirely on problems . . . can do as much damage as good."

Across the spectrum

Whether hosting local critique groups, touring to underserved communities, or volunteering with a larger and perhaps national organization, literary citizens have ample opportunity to share

9

In and Outside of Academia

Those already affiliated with an academic institution—instructors, alumni, and current students alike—may have a built-in community. Whether developing a writer's group or reading series in conjunction with campus programming, encouraging young writers through extracurricular literary activities, or working with peers outside of the school, all of these add up to possible opportunities for community enrichment. Nonacademics, however, needn't feel at a disadvantage.

Community colleges, in particular, are open to working with writers and other community members who wish to collaborate to offer one-time, month-long, or series programming. Most university campuses open doors to community members for specific writing events, often hosted on campus and available free to the public. Touring authors may approach campus programmers or English and Writing departments to suggest such events.

When Richard Bausch, whose writing has appeared in *Harper's*, *The New Yorker*, and *Esquire*, in addition to his dozens of books, joined the faculty at Chapman University in California, he offered a special workshop open only to members of the general public, rather than students who already have access to creative writing opportunities. The intent was to inspire interest and creativity in community members and provide a mentorship opportunity to those who might not otherwise have such encouragement. In the promotional material leading up to the workshop, Bausch said, "We don't put any limitations on applicants, either by age or by background. Who can tell where the next good writer will come from? A selected participant could be a high school student, unemployed, a doctor, a lawyer, a teacher, a custodian or restaurant worker, a retired person, a truck driver. Frankly, the more diversity in the class, the better."[1]

Literary citizens need not be best-selling authors or university professors to offer educational opportunities for developing writers. In celebration of National Library Week, Hagerstown Community College and the Washington County Public Library, both based in Hagerstown, Maryland, teamed up with local authors to provide free creative writing workshops at a local mall. The workshops included writing exercises and critiques, as well as a session on how to find an agent. A writer with even a handful of publications can offer to lead community workshops and be an inspiration to those who have just developed an interest in writing.

---

[1]Chapman University English Department, http://www.chapman.edu/wilkinson/english/writing-workshop.aspx.

Connecting through community education

Most community colleges are very eager to hear from community members who wish to offer talks, workshops, and reading groups. Authors may approach continuing education programmers with an idea for either a free or paid workshop, keeping in mind that community colleges wish to keep their programming as accessible as possible. In my own experience, local colleges rarely charge more than $30 for an intensive workshop, thereby keeping costs low for community members and increasing the potential audience.

Rhonda Hogrefe, a coordinator at Owens College in Ohio, says community colleges are "a perfect venue to offer classes for writing workshops because most writers, published or not, are looking for ways to polish their skills and give them an advantage in a very competitive market."

Hogrefe says community workshops encourage attendees to explore their own sense of style while learning about best practices in publishing, industry standards for submissions, and the finer details of specific genres. "Another advantage to writing workshops at the community college level is that in addition to the personal enrichment skills that students will acquire, they will also have the opportunity to gain professional development skills through group interaction and networking," she says, adding that such an environment provides an opportunity for building relationships with local peers.

Writers need not have an advanced degree to offer a workshop through a continuing education program. With a handful of publications, an outgoing and engaging speaker can share his or her skills with an audience that is just starting to explore their creative outlets. Hogrefe says that most community members who sign up to take community workshops are seeking "the opportunity to talk and learn from others who share their passion. Transferring thoughts into words is just the beginning of a successful writing journey. A writer can provide their will-set—commitment, creativity and work ethic—but the writing workshop can provide the skill-set—research, language, communication skills, and networking."

In less formal scenarios, community writers may work together to offer a special event focused on celebrating literary arts. Macomb Community College in Michigan has offered "A Day of Poetry," where area artists shared new writing, live music, and an open mic for the general public. Such an event may be spearheaded by anyone in the community with an interest in the arts. Even if you've never been an instructor, a local campus may be open to your proposal for reaching out to other community members with a shared interest in literature.

Fostering literary citizenship

Writers connected to academic programs might also use their built-in network to offer unique opportunities to those within and outside of the institution, as a means of connecting with the community. Outside of the formal academic environment, instructors have several opportunities to offer additional mentorship not only to their students, but also to the community at large.

The writing program at Ashland University, home of Ashland Poetry Press, has offered free 2-day workshops to community members during the month of December, making use of an otherwise quiet time on campus. Authors Deborah Fleming, Stephen Haven, Sarah M. Wells, and Lynn Powell recently teamed up to offer a weekend full of workshops, readings, publishing seminars, open mics, and casual conversation.

In a similar vein, students and faculty from the Iowa Writers' Workshop began the Iowa Youth Writing Project to share creative writing opportunities with at-risk or underprivileged youths. There was a mere handful of volunteers when the program began in 2010, but the number has blossomed to include more than 150 members working within the community and beyond, with the addition of volunteers from other institutions such as University of San Francisco. The program is not only a way for MFA students to incorporate community service in their studies, but also a way for members of the general public to assist in creating positive experiences for young writers. Community members are invited to get involved by submitting a volunteer application on its Web site iywp.org.

To help motivate and inspire future generations of literary citizens, author Cathy Day developed a credit course at Ball State University. While the syllabus for her special topics course "Literary Citizenship" also teaches students how to conduct themselves professionally, including offering guidance on submissions, querying agents and editors, and delivering public readings, Day encourages her class to contribute to the literary community around them. Lessons include how to build a writing community through social media, host author interviews and book reviews on blogs, and other tools to help students connect with others.

Day says her second offering of the course incorporated more time devoted to the book review section. "The first time I taught the course," she says, "they didn't try to publish them—other than on their own blogs—but that's because I didn't leave enough time to really introduce them to the practice and to the cultural value of book reviewing."

As shared on her Web site, Day says her approach to teaching creative writing is "not just to create more writers, per se, but to create a populace that values reading and writing, whatever form it takes."[2]

Other teacher-writers may find Day's course an inspiring model to introduce to their own institutions. Day says her initial pitch to administrators was well received. "Our curriculum at Ball State in creative writing has a special topics course built in. I'm teaching literary citizenship in that class," Day explains. "It would be more meaningful, I think, if the class officially became part of the curriculum, and that's a long term goal. . . . I expect that we'd have to really think about how the course fits into our overall program. The response so far from my colleagues and students has been very positive. For now, I'm happy teaching it once in awhile."

---

[2]Cathy Day homepage, cathyday.com.

Encouraging community engagement in academic settings needn't stem from formal classroom settings alone. Planting the seed of literary citizenship has been a priority for author Kaylie Jones. "The only thing I've ever asked my former students who've achieved commercial, critical, or simply literary recognition on any level, is to pay it forward and to help another writer in need of direction or advice," she says. "There is no more satisfying way to feel part of the writing community."

In her experience as a writing mentor, a number of her students have gone on to make volunteer work a regular part of their literary lives. Two such students have committed to working with inmates in a maximum facility prison. "These inmates are stunned by the help and attention they're receiving, absolutely free," she says, "and my former students are stunned by the emotional satisfaction they are getting from these attentive and driven writers. One of these prison writers has just had a story accepted in a major anthology. What could be more satisfying or emotionally fulfilling?"

Jones leads by example and she extends her own principles to working with the community. "For me personally, volunteering to teach high-school and middle-school age students to express their deepest feelings through writing was a saving grace in my early career as a writer. I always found that the toughest, hardest kid could be reached in this way," she says. "Volunteering in the schools, and later becoming a writer-in-residence in the schools through Teachers & Writers Collaborative, was one of the most important things I've ever done."

For those who already teach full-time, in addition to their own creative writing endeavors, time constraints can be a factor in how much and how often to contribute further to the community. Yet, like the community workshops discussed above, a literary citizen needn't offer a term-length class. Even a 1- or 2-hour workshop offered as a stand-alone event can provide wonderful opportunities to the community.

"Though teaching college classes full-time consumes most of my time, I do think it's important to give writing workshops in my community," says author Susan Tekulve. "I don't have as much time to do as much community outreach work as I would like, but usually I have plenty of opportunities every year to teach in alternative venues. . . . I generally enjoy teaching out in the community. I meet a lot of interesting people, and it's a way to help out those people who spend all of their waking hours working toward building a stronger sense of literary community in my town."

Outside the classroom

Other writing instructors, like Travis Nicholson, offer their time outside of the classroom to encourage students in their publication endeavors. At the University of Arkansas-Monticello, Nicholson offers his guidance to the student-run publication, *Foliate Oak*. He says this can be a rewarding experience, and the success of the journal is "very much tied to the student staff member." Instructors who volunteer to oversee such activities witness students grow as selective editors, while students gain practical experience that can be applied to their greater plans as writers.

This experience can be extended even after graduation. Students of the Northwest Institute of Literary Arts program, on Whidbey Island in Washington State, work with alumni to produce *Soundings Review*, a literary magazine founded in 2006. Submissions are open to writers throughout their immediate community and beyond, as program director Wayne Ude says, they've "always been aware of the larger community of writers in everything we do."

As part of its organizational mandate, which offers the only graduate writing program outside of a college or university, the association of writers also provides noncredit workshops in the local community. "We've consistently offered programs for every level of writer, whether those thinking about writing, beginning, intermediate, or advanced writers who enroll in a range of activities," Ude says.

Encouraging student writers to think about their greater communities is something Emma Bolden, a professor at Georgia Southern University, had in mind when she, in her own words, "decided to include a project in the class that would help them to express and share their love of the written word simply for the joy of it."

In 2010, she developed The Yawp, a poetry project in which she encourages people to share a well-loved poem on a sticky note, white board, or other medium and leave it in a public place. Bolden also asks that the person photograph where the poem was left and send it along with the story of how it got there, so that she may share these random acts of poetry on The Yawp blog. The result has included poems left in public venues such as workplace hallways, airport lounges, truck stops, and restrooms, all awaiting discovery by an unsuspecting passerby.

Bolden says the project began exclusively as a class assignment, but her students took the extra steps to make the project a public venture. "They taught me about what can happen when poetry becomes part of one's daily environment, whether that's a physical space or an online space. People posted poems on their Facebook profiles—an act that might at first seem minor, but, when the students explained that this was the first time most of their friends and family had seen the poems they'd been writing in secret, I realized what a major move that was on their parts," she says. "They taught me that excitement about poetry can be contagious. Poems started appearing across campus, in town, from people who weren't in my class and weren't even students. . . . It was an incredible experience to see so many people who were so very different, all involved in finding ways to put poetry out into the world."

What a student learns in and outside of the classroom most often has long-lasting effects when it comes to community engagement. John Proctor, online editor of *Hunger Mountain*, has been working with the journal since his second semester in the Vermont College of Fine Arts writing program. Since graduating with his MFA, he remains involved not only in the journal's production, but in the Vermont community as well, despite living in Brooklyn. Proctor says he is "spiritually connected" to his alma mater's home base.

"I have so many memories from summer residencies of the amazing local Fourth of July Parade and frolicking in swimming holes with a bunch of fellow pasty writers between workshops and lectures, and winter residencies drinking at the Three Penny Taproom and browsing the many used bookstores," Proctor says. "Living in Brooklyn as a writer can sometimes be daunting as it seems, in my neighborhood at least, that everyone is a writer or an artist or a musician or an actor, and many times when I'm feeling particularly faceless I think of my crowd in Montpelier and smile."

The continued connection to *Hunger Mountain* allows Proctor to contribute to the larger literary conversation, particularly through regular online articles and blog posts focused on literary citizenship. "I don't think *Hunger Mountain* is singular in having lots of craft and literary citizenship-based essays in our online incarnation—these are the type of things we writers love to share on our Facebook profiles and Twitter feeds after all! That said, we do spend a *lot* of editorial time and energy with our writers in conceptualizing and developing these pieces," Proctor says.

The author adds that he received guidance from Cynthia Newberry Martin and Claire Guyton during the development of a reviews series he was working on as a student. "This ended up serving as an informal apprenticeship with Cynthia and Claire, and I learned a lot of what I practice in my own editorial style from them," he says. "I think this is a pretty typical writer-editor relationship at *Hunger Mountain* for the meta-writing pieces—lots of conversation, multiple drafts, and hopefully discoveries along the way that translate for readers of the pieces they produce."

The result for Proctor, and the *Hunger Mountain* community, is a continuing series about literary citizenship, community engagement, and other related features that fall under their "Writing Life" Web section.

The alumni connection

One major benefit of studying in a formal program is the potential for making lifelong friends and colleagues. Whether graduate or undergraduate, the immersion of a few years spent together in workshops and lectures can forge lasting and meaningful bonds. Of course, it's up to the graduating writers to keep those connections alive by working together, either to sustain critique groups or to join forces for community enrichment.

Lillian-Yvonne Bertram, mentioned in the previous chapter for her service in underrepresented communities, continues to work with peers she met years ago. In their desire to encourage writing in their communities, they formed Line Assembly, "a collective of six emerging poets and artists who met as undergraduates in the creative writing program at Carnegie Mellon University and forged a lasting friendship over a mutual love for poetry and the literary arts," Bertram says.

As individuals, the writers have completed MFA degrees, published books, received awards, and taught at all levels, yet together they are able to combine passions and interests in serving the greater community. "While we all come from different places and backgrounds, we share an indebtedness to community experiences with poetry in our early childhoods and adolescence—most notably in branch libraries, writing groups, and independent bookstores that hosted readings and fostered grassroots literary activity."

Some grads connect over a shared interest in publishing emerging voices. Such is the case with the editors from *Split Infinitive*, a journal produced by graduates of the Pacific University MFA writing program. The team is an entirely volunteer operation and its mission is "to create a platform that promotes good literature while helping to build a community of writers."[3]

Other authors like Nicole Idar, a graduate of the George Mason writing program, offer to others in the community what was personally missed as an emerging writer. After she graduated, Idar says she recognized how important a community connection was to her and that her writing life was more than about the writing process alone. "Just like in many other professions where people volunteer their time, it's fulfilling to work on additional projects that I hope will benefit the writing community in some way," she says. "When I started out as a writer, I wasn't as well-informed as I wish I'd been. I was a financial journalist at the time, and I didn't know a single person who was a fiction writer. I'd never even published a short story in a national journal before I went to George Mason. When I graduated, it seemed to me that I'd learned things I wanted to be able to share with others."

While Idar was a student, she enjoyed the workshops available to her, volunteered with literary journal, and helped coordinate reading events, but she wasn't as mindful about the writing

---

[3]*Split Infinitive Digital Literary Magazine*, spiltinfinitive.com.

communities outside her immediate program. "It was only after I graduated that I thought hard about finding a way to form a writing community to sustain me outside school," she says. "So I decided I would reach out to other writers and put together panels about topics I wish I'd known more about when I was at school." This prompted the author to organize workshops at Politics & Prose, a bookshop in Washington DC, and at the Writer's Center in Bethesda. Idar gathered panelists from Johns Hopkins, University of Maryland, her alma mater, and local writers alike to share an open discussion with interested community writers.

Making it happen

Regardless of your own personal ties to an academic institution, there are countless ways to engage with formal writing programs, continuing education workshops, and community centers in an effort to provide mentorship and support to emerging writers. While there may be some advantages to having a built-in network of faculty and student peers, many of the activities mentioned in this chapter can just as easily be accomplished by a motivated community member.

Community colleges, as mentioned, are often welcoming starting points for potential workshop providers. Community education program developers most often request to see a brief workshop description, a list of projected learning outcomes, and an idea of the in-class activities participants will be asked to complete. You'll find that a good number of colleges provide a workshop proposal template on their Web sites, so start by checking what your local college has available to you. Then, a simple query to introduce who you are and what your idea is should be just the right tool to connect you with emerging community writers who can learn from your enthusiasm and experiences.

10

The Write Direction: Customizing your Community

Remember Walt Whitman's call to action? "Poets to Come" expresses the desire—no, the urgency—of passing on a legacy beyond one's own artistic presence. In combining a mindfulness of the future with the passion and action of our immediate care, today's literary citizens may carry out a vision not unlike Whitman's: to contribute to the now, but with a lasting impact on the future of our literary communities.

Literary acts of kindness need not be grand gestures. As we have seen from writers and readers throughout this book, there are countless ways to channel one's individual creativity and offer something valuable to others in our community. Whether that's showing up to support events hosted by peers, reviewing new small press titles, or organizing a fundraiser for a charitable organization, it's the quality of our engagement that matters.

While this book couldn't possibly showcase every example of contemporary literary citizenship in action, or point to every single group or organization that is doing something wonderful in the community, I do hope that the breadth of examples offered herein demonstrate this important point: literary citizenship is not exclusive, nor is it reserved for a specific group of writers or readers. Any person from any locale may engage in the community and offer something meaningful to others. As individuals, in every sense of the word, we bring something unique to the table when we work together to foster, sustain, and engage with the literary community for today—and for the future.

The myth of the solitary writer

We need one another. Sure, writers may be a bit reclusive when it comes to putting pen to paper, but even the most solitary writer needs to come up for air at some point. Writers need an audience, whether it's through a wide readership, a small community of peers, or even just one trusted reader. We desire to have our words read. And while we want our literary works to be a contribution in their own right, there is much joy to be had in connecting with others, in sharing in the successes of peers, and in contributing to the greater community around us.

The myths and legends of the solitary writing life may provide a romantic image to a developing writer—closing one's self off in a rustic cabin in the wilderness or spending solo sunny days in a small Parisian town—but even the most reclusive authors come out of hiding at some point if only to share their work with a potential reader.

In his acceptance speech for winning the Nobel Peace Prize in Literature in 1954, Ernest Hemingway famously said:

> Writing, at its best, is a lonely life. Organizations for writers palliate the writer's loneliness but I doubt if they improve his writing. For he does his work alone and if he is a good enough writer he must face eternity, or the lack of it, each day.[1]

Yet, even Hemingway, often looked upon as a poster-child for solitude in creativity, sought out a sense of place in his writing community. He was mentored by Gertrude Stein and Ezra Pound during his early years in Paris. He and James Joyce became good friends. And, of course, there is the famed love–hate relationship between Hemingway and Canadian writer Morley Callaghan. When not socking each other on the jaw, these two writers found common ground in literature, which inspired them to venture off to Paris where they forged friendships with other writers, including F. Scott Fitzgerald.

While solitude may provide a writer the space to think and create, author Wayne Ude suggests that many legends of solitary writers are more myth than reality. "Emily Dickenson is sometimes touted as a model of the solitary writer, but she sent her work out during her lifetime and tried for a mentee–mentorship

---

[1]Ernest Hemingway Banquet Speech, www.NobelPrize.org/nobel_prizes/literature/laureates/1954/hemingway-speech.html.

relationship with the editor of *Atlantic Monthly*," Ude says. "Even then, most writers sought out other writers. Sometimes they did so by heading for a college or university where a recognized writer lived."

Ude adds that many writers, like Hemingway and Callaghan, headed to major literary centers like London, Paris, Moscow, and New York in search of a creative community. "The procedure back then," he says, "seems to have gone something like this: move to the city, find out which taverns or bars the known writers were apt to frequent, and hang around."

Contemporary literary citizens needn't relocate to find the same sense of place and camaraderie as our literary legends did. Such a network may be found in your own small town or urban neighborhood, and even online through social networking sites. Community is yours to define and yours to expand.

The reluctant social butterfly

If you're a naturally shy person, you'll find comfort in knowing that most writers struggle to strike a balance between their introverted selves and their extroverted ambitions. "To be a successful writer, you have to have two very different skill sets," says author Loreen Niewenhuis. "One allows you to be alone and be productive writing and rewriting a book, the other side has to be social and able to engage an audience." The author says she "had the sit-at-the-desk-and-write thing down, but really had to develop the other skill set." Niewenhuis found her comfort zone while in the MFA program at Spalding University, where she was required to present readings to her graduating class. The experience boosted her confidence, and she took those skills and transferred them to her community activity.

Susan Tekulve, author of *In The Garden of Stone*, faced a similar challenge. "I am, by nature, an extremely shy person, but I'm also an extrovert," she says. "I crave long spaces of time alone, and I need this quietness and space for my work. But I also need to be around other people from time to time." Like many writers, Tekulve balances her writing profession with teaching, and even being in front of a classroom took her time to adjust. "I've had to train myself to be at ease with public speaking."

Immersing one's self in the support of a writing community can ease the anxiety of speaking in front of an audience, boost one's confidence for public readings, and provide opportunities for pushing one's boundaries. In the best of situations, that confidence transfers to the rest of your writing life and pushes you to be the best writer you can be. A community can provide inspiration and motivation for those gloomy days that all writers inevitably face. From time to time, we all need the support and kinship of fellow writers and readers to give us a creative boost. Offering our fellow community members that same sense of support can provide an even greater rush in knowing that we, too, have something to give to others.

Random acts of kindness

In writing, as in life, sometimes it's the little things that make a big impact. One small kind gesture can provide a smile on someone else's face for the rest of the day; one tiny nod of support can make another feel like all the downs are worth the ups.

Like the "charming notes" author Carolyn See[2] encourages us to write and send to others every day, a small, but genuine literary act of kindness is a great way to contribute to your community, near and far. That may be sharing a social media link to a peer's new book, sending a thank you note to an editor who took the time to offer personal feedback on a submission, offering to help a writer promote his or her upcoming event, or taking gently used books to a donation drop-off center where others may access literature. We all have an opportunity to do a little good every day. We can all find occasions to give even just one moment of our time and appreciation for what others are doing, and what others need, in our communities.

Here's a shining example of what a simple gesture can do to lift another's spirits. On the Facebook page for BookEnds, the literary agency shared this post:

Recently Jessica Faust got her first piece of fan mail. A reader of cozy mysteries emailed to say that she always reads the acknowledgments in books and noticed many of her favorite authors had mentioned Jessica as their agent. And then she thanked Jessica for standing behind the authors and "helping their books make their way into our hands and our lives." Jessica was supremely touched by this email. It says everything about why she loves her job so much. So for today,

[2]Carolyn See, *Making A Literary Life* (Random House, 2002), 37.

we at BookEnds are all going to make an effort to commit a random act of thank you, by reaching out to someone just to say thank you for all that you do.[3]

This is a fine example of how reaching out to one person may inspire another to do so, with the mindset of paying such kindness forward in the community.

Everyday inspiration

What better way to find inspiration than through others. More and more, journals and online publications are recognizing the power of influence in showcasing contemporary literary citizens and their efforts. It's hard not to feel compelled to take action when one reads about another person doing something for the benefit of others. Kindness and generosity are most often contagious. Think about this in terms of daily life: When someone holds a door open for you, are you not more likely to return the gesture to another? Likewise, when a person allows the door to slam in your face, does it not leave a lingering emotion? This same cause and effect can be applied to your literary life. We can't help but react positively when we see others acting as such.

On the *Ploughshares* Web site a few years ago, author Laura van den Berg hosted "Innovators in Literature." This 15-part series interviewed authors, publishers, and other active community

---

[3]BookEnds Literary Agency on Facebook, www.facebook.com/BookEndsLlc.

members who were somehow contributing to the community beyond their own writing. The interviews often included ideas and inspirations for how readers could get involved, take a lead, and put to use their own creative energies in their respective communities. In turn, there was a positive reaction from readers who posted in the blog comment section, but even more shared the link through social media channels and carried on the discussion off-site.

"Reading literary blogs and participating in comment conversations is a great way to connect to other writers," says author Roxane Gay. "Twitter feels like a great big nerd cafeteria. I also enjoy the writing community on Tumblr. It can feel overwhelming trying to figure out where you belong, where you can fit in, but the great thing about most writing communities is that you can create your own place within them. In creating opportunities for others, share what you know. There's no need to hoard what you know about craft or community."

LitBridge is an online venue that's doing exactly that. The resource Web site, which has a mission of connecting writers with opportunities around the country, uses its social media and blog to promote community engagement, provide inspiration, and offer a venue for writers and readers to connect over their love of literature. Finding these online platforms and bookmarking them for updates can add an extra dose of inspiration to your day and perhaps motivate you to take action in your own personal way.

On an individual level, West Virginia writer Diane Tarantini uses social media to connect with her local writing community. "Our state writing group, West Virginia Writers, has a lively

Facebook page," she says. "Folks post dozens of times a day—encouraging one another, announcing literary events, and putting up links to craft articles. We have over 750 members and I check this page a couple times a day."

For author Jeanetta Calhoun Mish, whose books include *Work is Love Made Visible*, book reviewing is where she finds inspiration. "For me, review writing is a creative endeavor, one that also allows me to improve my own craft by teasing out how others bring poems or stories into the world. Writing reviews also teaches me to be a better editor, because the process forces me to confront the writing on its own grounds." She adds that "writing reviews allows us to join in the literary conversation, no matter where we live."

Lee Herrick, author of *Gardening Secrets of the Dead*, uses the social time at in-person events like readings and book signings to engage with the community on a deeper level. "I value the human connections that can arise from a book signing," he says. "The rewards nourish me—talking before or after a reading with a student whose curiosity about language begins to bloom, a prize-winning author whose work I have admired, or a Korean adoptee hearing poems to which she can relate for the first time in her life. There are many good ways a poet can engage with the public—online, curating events and supporting other poets—but what I find most rewarding are authentic conversations that spawn friendships with other writers, new audiences, and people from all backgrounds who find common ground after hearing a poem."

While this book demonstrates a variety of ways to emerge one's self in the community and contribute to the literary lives of others, there is no need to start from scratch or reinvent the proverbial wheel. As a book lover, you're no doubt already active in the community in some regard. Consider what you are already doing and how you might be able to enhance your community participation.

Goal setting

In addition to the examples shared within these chapters, the appendix offers a small sampling of additional organizations and groups that consistently rely on the support of others. You may already belong to one or more organizations, associations, or local groups. What can you offer beyond your membership dues? Chances are that the organization has opportunities for participating on a committee, assisting with fundraising events, helping with awareness campaigns, or hosting events.

While the examples of literary citizenship herein hopefully offer inspiration and motivation to reach out to your community, only *you* can determine the extent of your involvement. Managing your time, energy, and resources is necessary in order to ensure that you can sustain your efforts—no doubt while writing, working the day job, and tending to your social life and family.

Once you have given thought to realistic time commitments and determined what you can offer to others, consider the following options for enhancing your community engagement:

If you're already a part of a critique group, start there. Why not organize a reading to showcase your local authors? You can add an open mic segment to encourage public participation.

What other authors and groups are local to your area and what events do they have coming up? How can you help a fellow writer launch his or her book or organize a reading? Perhaps you can collaborate with others to give a talk at a local school. Consider bringing literature to the mainstream by offering an inspirational noon hour chat at your workplace or for your local small business association or chamber of commerce.

Perhaps it's been years since you've touched base with your fellow alums. Why not organize an informal alumni reunion, either on or off campus?

What are your favorite literary journals? Contact those who run such journals for contributing a book review or ask them how you can volunteer. You may be able to lend a hand with reading slush piles submissions, updating their Web site or blog, or assisting with fundraising or subscription drives.

Most importantly: Write. Read. Share your passion with others. Mentor emerging writers and show appreciation to those in your community. Let others know when they have moved you or motivated you in some way, big or small. Find everyday moments that inspire you and extend that kindness to another.

Give your time freely and with passion only when your schedule allows. After all, giving should be a gift for both you and the recipient.

Balance and sustainability

"First and foremost, literary citizenship is about the writing," says author Susan Tekulve. "This sounds obvious, but what I mean by this is that to experience true literary citizenship you have to be serious about the writing. It has to be something you do every day, even when you are tired or worn out from the job you have to work to pay your bills."

This is sage advice. Being an active member of the community can be a rewarding experience. When a reading event goes well, when a community event draws in an impressive crowd, or when a start-up literary journal garners attention from a sizeable readership, all of these things are worth celebrating. The rush of adrenaline that comes with seeing something through to success is undeniable.

But, giving to others can also be addictive. Such a result is only worrisome when one's writing begins to take a back seat to others' needs. "Most writers burn out on community involvement from time to time," says author Wayne Ude. "In my experience, those who enjoy attending but not assisting with writers' gatherings, readings, celebrations of the most recent state or regional literary awards and so on, tend not to burn out. Rather, it's those who arrange or lead such activities who are apt to exhaust themselves."

It's necessary to keep the act of writing a priority. Involvement in the community should supplement, but not replace, one's writing ambitions. Ude says, "For many of us, sitting down with the laptop or notebook or even tape recorder is the hardest part of writing: that is, keeping up the daily commitment to write just as an accountant keeps up the daily commitment to open a spreadsheet. Once we've made that first move, we're apt to stick with it until words of some sort are down on the page, no matter how desperately they'll need revision."

Taking an active role in community events can provide a break from the creative work, but Ude suggests that writers surround themselves with peers who will be protective of one another's writing time. "Any leadership position will offer constant opportunities to put off writing to accomplish some immediate task on behalf of the community," he says. "It's a difficult temptation to resist, especially because that sort of work offers another sort of creativity: the opportunity to build something of value to the community of writers. With luck, one's fellow writers will stage an intervention."

Author Gale Martin limits her acts of literary citizenship to specific events and to a defined amount of online support for writers. This has been helpful in providing balance between work and play, but even more so when the author was moving to a new city and starting a new job. "Those demands combined are exhausting, and no one can write when she is exhausted mentally and physically," she says. By focusing on specific events and peer support she can control, Martin is able to give back without sacrificing too much. "I just find that investing in other people pays dividends—in every conceivable way. In terms of putting boundaries around my involvement, it helps that I only profile other writers on my blog once a week at most."

Loreen Niewenhuis takes a similar approach to managing her time between the community and her personal writing needs. The author reserves the first few months of the year exclusively for writing. This hibernation time allows her to focus on works-in-progress, while also looking forward to events in the future. "If I get requests, I slide them into April or later in the year. These three months are protected for my writing," she says. "I'm much more productive that way." When Niewenhuis is on the road for a book tour, she dedicates her mornings to writing to ensure that her creative needs are met even during a busy schedule.

Author and editor Roxane Gay agrees that it's important to put one's creative needs first. "I am not sure how I balance everything, but I always make time for my own writing because writing is what relaxes me and what I enjoy most." She adds, "I never want to forget I'm a person and a writer before I'm anything else."

Yet when a writer takes on a leadership role, as Ude suggests, it can be difficult to defend the time needed for personal space. Poet Alex Boyd, author of *Making Bones Walk*, is the founding editor of *Northern Poetry Review*. Over the years, he has discovered that working with the right people makes all the difference when it comes to time management. "I was lucky enough to find reviewers who produce a finished review that often needs very little changed, and I'd say that's extremely valuable. But even so, it takes time away from your own writing and other projects, in finding moments to encourage reviews, edit, and post them." Boyd says managing a journal includes a lot of behind-the-scenes tasks that potential editors may not realize or account for in their plans for a start-up. Those who are considering starting a journal, even if online, can benefit from the involvement and support from others who are willing to share the workload while taking advantage of the creative opportunity.

For some writers, being involved in the community is a necessary part of their creative process. Author Susan Tekulve spent 8 years writing *In The Garden of Stone*, yet she sought support from peers as the project came to an end. She says, "I felt a kind of grief. There is no other word for this. The novel was done, and I felt exhausted and somewhat bereft, like I'd told every story I ever needed to tell. The well was definitely dry. Also, I was sending the book around for publication, which is a whole different kind of strain that can keep you from feeling like writing." As she came to terms with feeling creatively blocked, Tekulve immersed herself in a number of other creative outlets to rejuvenate. "I kept reading. I took Italian language classes. I read a lot of books on Sicily, which is the setting for the book I thought I wanted to write next. I wrote some essays. I wrote book reviews."

Yet, it was in commiserating with other writers who shared similar experiences that Tekulve found comfort. "In short, I had a very long and restless period during which I drove everyone, including myself, crazy because I wasn't writing. But I had a lot of writer friends who had experienced the same thing after they finished their first novels, and they were there to tell me that what I was feeling and experiencing was pretty typical."

One peer in particular shared her own frustrations with writer burn-out and publication woes. This writer "confessed that she felt the same grief, the same loss, the same inertia every time she finished one book, before she started a new book," Tekulve says. "She advised me to keep taking Italian classes and to work on tidying up: completing short essays and stories while I continued to send out the novel manuscript. This was very sound advice, and definitely an example of good literary citizenship, of how it works at its best."

Tekulve discovered what others may when feeling connected to others in the community. The art of writing is a solitary act, but it is in the support of others, in the encouragement shared by writing peers and community members, that much of our anxiety about the creative work may be placated.

Engagement with other writers comes natural to many of us. It may not always be planned or strategically thought out in how we connect with others. It needn't be. Yet, there are some incredible opportunities for tending to our community in more formal modes, perhaps through an organization or through grassroots efforts. While the job of the writer is to write and focus on honing the craft, we all need the same thing from one another. We all benefit from support and encouragement, no matter where we are in our literary journey.

Helping emerging writers develop their voice, supporting what our peers are doing, and cheering on the successes of even those we don't know personally needn't be time consuming— and shouldn't be seen as a burdensome task. As many of these authors have demonstrated, literary citizenship is most beneficial to others when it is an authentic act, one that comes naturally to our regular lives. Sometimes, though, we need to see examples. We need to hear inspiring stories from real people. I hope, through the discussions and examples within these chapters, you have perhaps been inspired to try something new, reach out a little further into your community, and share your skills, talents, and time with others in ways that will offer them as much joy as it will for you, as well. As Whitman recognized in "Poets to Come," it is our mindfulness of others that encourages growth and possibility in our literary community.

Appendix A: Community Organizations

This list of organizations offers a mere sampling of the many places where writers and readers can work together for bettering their literary communities. Whether working on a regional or national level, these organizations rely on volunteers and/or active members to offer time, energy, and ideas in carrying out their respective goals.

There are even more community groups, both formal and grassroots, spread out across the country and beyond. Some of these are listed on the *Poets & Writers* Web site in a database of "Literary Places." This resource provides a searchable list of literary venues where writers and readers can connect with the community. You'll find that resource at pw.org/literary_places. If you're looking for a local writers' group, *The Writer Magazine* hosts a searchable database at writermag.com/groups.aspx. And while there are any number of online resources to connect you with others, most of the organizations listed below offer both in-person and online opportunities for contributing to the community.

49 Alaska Writing Center offers a community blog, an events series, writing workshops, a youth program, and also coordinates Alaska Book Week. http://49writingcenter.org

826 National is a nonprofit organization that provides leadership, administration, and other resources to ensure the success of its network of regional writing and tutoring centers. The centers offer a variety of programs that provide underresourced students, aged 6–18, with opportunities to explore their creativity and improve their writing skills. http://826national.org

The Academy of American Poets supports American poets at all stages of their careers and fosters the appreciation of contemporary poetry. Programs include a book club, online poetry classroom, a resource center, and the sponsorship of National Poetry Month. http://www.poets.org

Association of Writers & Writing Programs (AWP) provides support, advocacy, resources, and community to nearly 50,000 writers, 500 college and university creative writing programs, and 125 writers' conferences and centers. Its mission is to foster literary achievement, advance the art of writing as essential to a good education, and serve the makers, teachers, students, and readers of contemporary writing. https://www.awpwriter.org

Canadian Creative Writers and Writing Programs is a professional organization devoted to supporting the teaching of creative writing. Programs include a national conference, online networking forums, and pedagogical resources for those teaching creative writing. http://www.ccwwp.ca

Canadian Women in the Literary Arts (CWILA) promotes strong and active female perspectives and presences within the Canadian literary landscape. http://cwila.com

Cave Canem is committed to cultivating the artistic and professional growth of African-American poets. Programs include a lecture series, workshops, and retreats. http://www.cavecanem poets.org

City Lit Project connects readers and writers across Maryland through public events, workshops, and community collaboration. http://www.citylitproject.org

Gemini Ink, in San Antonio TX, nurtures readers and writers through Writers In Communities, a program that sends professional writers into the community to offer free workshops for students of all ages and abilities. http://geminiink.org

Girls Write Now offers mentorship for at-risk and underserved girls from New York City's public high schools. http://www.girls writenow.org

Great Lakes Commonwealth of Letters is a nonprofit organization in Grand Rapids MI with a mission to encourage, promote, and celebrate the literary endeavors of writers within the Great Lakes region. Programs include readings, workshops, and community outreach. http://readwritelive.org

Grub Street is a nonprofit writing center dedicated to nurturing writers and connecting readers throughout the Boston area. http://www.grubstreet.org

The Hudson Valley Writers' Center in Sleepy Hollow NY includes programming to advance the art and craft of writing among diverse communities. http://www.writerscenter.org

Just Buffalo Literary Center has a mission to create and strengthen communities through the literary arts. Its aim is to foster a community that supports and values reading, writing, and the transformative power of literary arts. Programs include a critique group, a Writers in Education Program, an open mic series for youth, and a lecture series. http://www.justbuffalo.org

Lighthouse Writers Workshop is an independent literary center in Denver CO. Services include year-round workshops, a summer Lit Fest, and youth programs. https://lighthousewriters.org

Literary Arts is a community-based nonprofit literary center located in downtown Portland that serves Oregon's readers and writers. Activities include lectures, discussion groups, and a Writers in the Schools program. http://www.literary-arts.org

The Loft Literary Center, located in Minneapolis MN, serves 600,000 individuals every year with classes, festivals, and youth programming. https://www.loft.org

The Maine Writers & Publishers Alliance is a nonprofit organization dedicated to enriching the literary life and culture of Maine. Activities include Poetry Express, a community reading and discussion program. http://mainewriters.org

The Muse Writers Center provides a resource and community center for the Norfolk VA area, and hosts events and seminars for writers of all ages and experiences. http://www.the-muse.org

The Neighborhood Writing Alliance provokes dialogue, builds community, and promotes change by creating opportunities for adults in Chicago's underserved neighborhoods to write, publish, and perform works about their lives. It aims to connect adults through creative communities in which writing, discussing, and publishing personal narrative lead to civic engagement, neighborhood vitality, and social transformation. http://www.jot.org

The New Hampshire Writers' Project is a nonprofit organization that serves as a resource for writers, publishers, booksellers, literary agents, educators, librarians, and readers in and near New Hampshire. Programs include a monthly gathering for writers, book clubs throughout the state, social events, workshops, and an annual festival. http://www.nhwritersproject.org

The North Carolina Writers' Network serves writers through programs that offer ample opportunities for professional growth in skills and insight. The organization builds audiences for literature, advocates for the literary arts and for literacy, and provides information and support services. http://www.ncwriters.org

PEN American Center is a membership association that seeks to defend the freedom of expression wherever it may be threatened, and promote and encourage the recognition and reading of contemporary literature. http://www.pen.org

The Poetry Center at Passaic County Community College, in Paterson NJ, has a mission to promote poets and poetry and to bring poetry to a wider and more diverse audience. http://www.pccc.edu/home/cultural-affairs/poetry-center

The Poetry Society of America, the nation's oldest poetry organization, has a mission to build a larger and more diverse audience for poetry, to encourage a deeper appreciation of the vitality and breadth of poetry in the cultural conversation, and to place poetry at the crossroads of American life. http://www.poetrysociety.org

Poets House is a national poetry library and literary center open to poets and the public. Its mission is to stimulate public dialogue on issues of poetry in culture. Programs include Poetry at Large, a public poetry series, as well as exhibitions, readings, and workshops for all ages. http://poetshouse.org

The Prisoner Express program, sponsored by the Durland Alternatives Library in Ithaca NY, promotes rehabilitation by offering inmates resources and opportunities for creative self-expression. http://prisonerexpress.org

The Ragdale Foundation is a nonprofit artists' community located just outside of Chicago IL. In addition to community programming and writers' workshops, it offers school programs for middle school, high school, and college classes. http://www.ragdale.org

San Diego Writers, Ink is a nonprofit organization offering groups, workshops, and services for the literary community throughout San Diego County. http://www.sandiegowriters.org

Seattle Arts & Lectures presents community programs that foster diverse ideas, the imagination, and a love of reading and writing. Programs include a lecture series and Writers in the Schools program. http://lectures.org

She Writes is an online community and virtual workplace for women who write across the genres. The organization includes online discussion groups, collaborations in local communities, educational programming, and an independent press. http://www.shewrites.com

StoryStudio Chicago offers discussion groups, workshops, and a creative space to encourage writers of all ages and experiences. The Words for Work program offers creative support to members of the business community. http://www.storystudio chicago.com

The Virginia G. Piper Center for Creative Writing, housed at Arizona State University, aspires to foster a thriving creative and literary community, promote the accessibility of art in the community, and offer a creative environment for the Arizona and global communities. http://www.asu.edu/piper

Thurber House is a nonprofit literary center in Columbus OH. It offers educational and community programs including Summer Literary Picnics and camps for children. http://www.thurber house.org

VIDA: Women in Literary Arts seeks to explore critical and cultural perceptions of writing by women through conversation and the exchange of ideas among existing and emerging literary communities. http://www.vidaweb.org

World Book Night is an annual celebration dedicated to spreading the love of reading, person to person. Volunteers across the country go into their communities to give away half a million books to light and nonreaders. http://www.us.worldbooknight. org

Writers & Books began in 1974 as The Book Bus, a mobile bookstore and distributor that traveled throughout the northeastern United States. The organization now houses a community reading program, writing resource center, and youth programs. http://www.wab.org

The Writer's Center, a nonprofit organization operated out of Maryland, offers workshops and community engagement for writers within the local area as well as online. http://www. writer.org

The YMCA National Writer's Voice is a network of independent literary arts centers hosted at YMCAs across the country. It offers accessible and community-driven literary arts programming. http://writerscenter.tripod.com/dwc/id2.html

Appendix B: Sample Book Reviews

Book reviewing, as described in Chapter 6, is one of the easiest ways to contribute to the greater literary community. For invested readers, it need only take an additional day or two to formulate and share one's critical response to a book worthy of additional exposure.

To complement the advice and sample query letters already included in Chapter 6, the following four reviews should help demonstrate the basics of writing compelling reviews. Thanks to the reviewers and the respective publishers for sharing these published examples with readers. While there is no single way to go about reviewing a book, it is advised to follow the submission guidelines of each target market prior to submitting.

Companion Grasses, poetry
by Brian Teare
Review by Jacqueline Lyons
Originally published October 2013
Colorado Review/Colorado State University
Center for Literary Publishing[1]

In *Companion Grasses*, Brian Teare embodies the definition of poet as daydreamed by Thoreau while "Walking," the poet who would transplant words "to his page with earth adhering to their roots . . . who could impress the winds and streams into his service, to speak for him." Teare sustains a philosophical-linguistic dance-conversation with Thoreau, Dickinson, Emerson, and others contemporary and ancestral, literary and familial; he produces original and authentic art as he adheres to origins. Consider the delight in "Little Errand":

> I gather the rain
>
> in both noun
> & verb. The way
>
> the river banks
> its flood, floods
> its banks, quiver's
>
> grammar I carry

---

[1]Jacqueline Lyons, "*Companion Grasses* by Brian Teare," Colorado State University Center for Literary Publishing, October 2013, http://coloradoreview.colostate.edu/reviews/companion-grasses.

The book's arrangement into three distinct sections feels intentional and intuitive, while remaining collaborative with content. The poems in part one are particularly resonant of a naturalist's guide, and have the effect of illuminating without mediating— the best guide helps us see with our own eyes. As the poet surveys, he impresses rural and urban landscape into his service; they help him speak, or he helps them. Physical landscape shapes poetic form—text on open field pages echoes edges and ocean, rivulets and hillocks and ledges. Land or ocean or idea offers, and Teare meets it in "White Graphite/(*Limantour Beach*)":

> the spit's edge open
> to ocean goes pure
>
> contour: absence
> of light, self's how
>
> a tern's clutch nests
> in next to nothing:
>
> beach without moon
> mere rumor, blur's
> texture a scumble
>
> scoured of color:
>
> . . .
>
> matter a mere shift
> in limits, even skin's
>
> a trick of the liminal:

This opening poem holds much of the book's explorations in microcosm: precise arrangement of words and lines; form reflecting content (here, spare language sketches images and concepts of edge and space); a glimpse of the elegiac to come; language as extension of thought and/or thought as extension of sound; and an introduction to one of the theoretical threads pursued across the book (the relationship between matter and spirit).

A summer walk offers, as in "Quakinggrass/(*Briza Maxima*)," and Teare braids multiple perspectives, "not collage exactly," into a poem that combines landscape with language and biology: "Gnats hovered above dirt/path between chaparral/(pretty word—Spanish—'evergreen oak'—". After isolating personal and ecological threads, Teare entwines them with theory as the speaker walks alongside an unnamed "he" whose "storied thigh/scarred just so . . . & tilted toward me": "I followed him— / no one had said 'love' yet— / high bluff cliffing the Pacific . . . ('a detail overwhelms//Entirety,' writes Barthes)—". The poem weds etymology and translation with attraction, weds landscape with theory, as varied in its spatial arrangements and mechanics as in its content, and ends/arrives at:

Little grammar of attraction—

Inflorescence—
(What is "lyric")—

The book fell open on its broken spine

(*florere*, "to flower")—
"It's quakinggrass," I said—

When Emily Dickinson was down, her lexicon was her companion. Here, too, where phenomena's best expression comes in terms of absence—"not collage exactly," not love "yet"—and suggests larger absences—it is language that provides structure and shelter. The speaker wants "to get / closer to where material / touches language", wants "two grammars to / marry the mutable to fundament."

In part two, the center of *Companion Grasses*, rests Teare's "Transcendental Grammar Crown": a gem-studded crown that opens with five epigraphs, one each by Emily Dickinson, Margaret Fuller, Charles Ives, Emerson, and Thoreau—invocations for the carefully shaped musing that follows. The sequence, a laurel of fifteen poems, fourteen lines each, weaves signature insights in a mode both critically engaging and laudatory, perhaps as consolation for other facts, or death, or the fact of death. The sequence is part prayerful garland, part homage, part smart literary love note. The poems are not mimetic of the work by those invoked in the epigraphs—rather more ekphrastic in how they speak out across time and space and genre to connect with ideas, more synchronized as in breathing with. It's a pleasure to witness Teare give these ideas additional faces and forms, as in the beginning of the paean "What's / (—)" to Dickinson and her signature dash and slant rhyme:

as saint
is slant
to pain

storm norm numb null
thorn pressed to thumb

The poems in this section are further woven together by echo and repetition of the last line of each poem to the first line of next, so that the poem that contains strands of Emerson's "Oversoul," and ends with the words "sweeter than seeing," is followed by a poem entitled "Vision Is Question"; and the last lines of the last poem, ". . . the leap from matter / to a transcendental grammar," harken back to the first poem, "Leap From Matter." In the end, it seems it's the Thoreauvian more than the Emersonian brand of transcendentalism held aloft. The poems' power to convey the spiritual comes from forms in the natural world, and love of those physical forms, despite or because they are ephemeral, as in "Star Thistle/(*Centaurea solstitialis*)," dedicated to Reginald Shepherd (April 10, 1963–September 10, 2008):

the thistle is not metaphor

& extends into the future
as far as I can see, easily filling the field I love:

. . .

& the wild deer in us were released at last
at dusk to disappear into the stand of manzanita far across
    the field I love:

The book contains a weave of praise, consolation, critical inquiry, and lamentation. The critical inquiry is not found exclusively in the more essayistic poems, nor is the mourning limited to the book's two final poems, one dedicated to the poet's father, one to poet Reginald Shepherd. It is a distinct feature of this book that it impresses into service both logic and passion, and that it can sustain a nerdy delight in physical artifacts alongside metaphysical meditations.

Thoreau, in his relative solitude at Walden, which is to say his self and spiritual exploration, speaks of the impossibility of loneliness (and perhaps the impossibility of endless mourning) when he writes that in his solitude "Every little pine needle expanded . . . with sympathy and befriended me." A similar suggestion and inherent argument is made in Brian Teare's *Companion Grasses*, which renews intimacy with language, fact, landscape, literature, and everyday feeling—such rich company.

If a Stranger Approaches You, fiction
by Laura Kasischke
Review by B. J. Hollars
Originally published Spring 2014, Issue 15
Los Angeles Review[2]

In her debut collection of stories, National Book Critics Circle Award winner and Guggenheim recipient Laura Kasischke proves her mettle beyond the poetry and novels that have drawn her such acclaim. In her latest effort, she reveals her prowess for the short story as well, producing a piercing collection filled with characters suffering from heartache, uncertainty, and a desire to violate the privacy of others. The latter is examined most closely in the opening story, in which a mother rationalizes the importance of snooping through her daughter's dresser drawers. Yet what she discovers is far more shocking than could ever be expected— a punishment of sorts for the trespass of violating a sacred trust. The theme of violated trust returns in the collection's final story as well, in which a stranger approaches a woman about [to] carry a package onto a plane. There, in the crowded terminal, the woman is forced to pit instinct against logic, compassion against fear, all while enduring her own private struggle of leaving her sick child behind. Time and again, Kasischke forces her characters into these crisis-packed situations, creating dilemmas that demand her characters confront their truest selves. Such is the case in

---

[2]B. J. Hollars, "*If a Stranger Approaches You* by Laura Kasischke." *Los Angeles Review* 15 (2014): 157–8.

"Melody," the collection's centerpiece, which places a father and soon-to-be ex-husband as a guest at his daughter's birthday party. The story juxtaposes Tony and Melody's current situation alongside their early days—an effective technique that reveals how simply and unexpectedly a blossoming love story became a cautionary tale. While Kasischke's premises always engage, they serve merely as entry points for the deep psychological probing soon to take place. In one scene, after Tony drops his daughter's birthday present, he glances around for signs that his lack of marital bliss has somehow become public as a result of his butterfingers. "Everything was fine," the narrator assures. "Nothing out of the ordinary here." On the whole, Kasischke's collection seeks to subvert this: Though little is out of the ordinary, clearly, not everything is fine.

The Art of Intimacy: The Space Between,
nonfiction by Stacey D'Erasmo
Review by B. J. Hollars
Originally published Spring 2014, Issue 15
Los Angeles Review[3]

In the latest installment of *The Art of* Series, novelist Stacey D'Erasmo explores intimacy as it applies to modern fiction. "What is the nature of intimacy," D'Erasmo asks in the book's opening line, "of what happens in the space between?" She approaches her study of the emotional lives of fictional characters by way of meditation rather than how-to guide, making clear early on that there is no magic bullet to creating deeply rooted bonds between characters. There are "as many ways of rendering intimacy as there are of being intimate . . ." D'Erasmo writes, and through her careful study of the works of Calvino, Conrad, Larsen, Lawrence and more, D'Erasmo reveals at least a few of them. While D'Erasmo's literature lecture offers astute observations, on occasion its opacity proves alienating for those unfamiliar with the texts. Yet in most instances, she provides powerful insight, most notably in her dissection of intimacy as it applies to a pivotal scene in Nella Larsen's novel, *Passing.* When two African-American childhood friends reunite in a Chicago tearoom, both are attempting to "pass"

---

[3]B. J. Hollars, "*The Art of Intimacy: The Space Between* by Stacey D'Erasmo." *Los Angeles Review* 15 (2014): 160.

themselves off as white, though only one recognizes the attempt in the other. "In the space between them," D'Erasmo writes, "a space as thin as a coin edge, is a vast, nearly unsayable realm of uncertainty . . ." Yet as D'Erasmo proves throughout, intimacy is often the result of what isn't said, of what needn't be said, of a closeness the readers feel but don't see.

This Assignment Is So Gay: LGBTIQ Poets on the Art of Teaching, anthology edited by Megan Volpert
Review by Elizabeth Kate Switaj
Originally published July 2013
Poets' Quarterly[4]

What stands out most about *This Assignment Is So Gay: LGBTIQ Poets on the Art of Teaching* is the diversity of perspectives, subjects, and, to a lesser degree, forms and styles it contains. An anthology that exceeds 200 pages will, of necessity, contain some variety, especially when each poet contributes three poems at most. In this case, however, variation becomes a stance: the alphabet soup of LGBTIQ cannot be reduced to a single subject or position. The boundaries of queerness are not easy to patrol or to define.

What emerges from this anthology, then, is not a single ideology or program for education but a multiplicity of voices and ideas. In the introduction, editor Megan Volpert states that "[t]he very existence of an LGBTIQ-identified teacher in the classroom is still an act of revolution" yet not every poem that follows supports the notion that the revolutionary potential of teaching-while-queer is always fulfilled. Hadar Ma'ayan, in "On Being a Queer Middle School Teacher," describes the pressures

---

[4]Elizabeth Kate Switaj, "*This Assignment Is So Gay: LGBTIQ Poets on the Art of Teaching* edited by Megan Volpert," *Poets' Quarterly*, July 2013, www.poetsquarterly. com/2013/07/this-assignment-is-so-gay-lgbtiq-poets.html.

and fears that lead some queer teachers to remain at least semi-closeted, causing them to miss out on teachable moments, as when a student, having been given a detention, retaliates with "I know you're a lesbian":

> In that moment of choice, I could have said, "She's right"
> Or "Let's discuss"
> Or "Does anybody have any questions?"
> But instead the fear rose in me.

The speaker's lesbianism does not disappear in this instant, but neither does it lead her to act any differently than a straight teacher might. The radical possibilities of queerness do not exempt queer teachers from the same kinds of pressures that non-queer teachers face but, in fact, makes these pressures more acute. Any teacher might be accused by a student of behaving in a way that would outrage parents and administrators. Any teacher might thus have her job threatened. For queer teachers, however, such accusations involve their very identities. Any discussion of how to bring the radical possibilities of queerness to bear in the classroom must, therefore, discuss the forces that constrain them; describing these pressures, as *This Assignment Is So Gay* does, gives such conversations a place to begin without prescribing solutions that might impose limits on queer teaching.

By avoiding consistent ideological stances, this anthology resists restraining the possibilities of queer pedagogy. Even the idea that "[o]f course 'it gets better'" with which Volpert begins her introduction does not always hold true. Insecurity and impostor syndrome recur as themes throughout the anthology, as the titles of Roma Raye's "Big Fat Faker" and Sarah-Jean Krahn's "Symptomatology of an Impostor" indicate. Shannon Parker's untitled poem follows the thoughts of a lesbian teacher who ends up "feeling / like a middle school student / instead of a teacher," embarrassed and ashamed when she hears students describe her sexuality negatively, while Daniel Gonzales' untitled piece tells us that "A teacher's lounge is no different / Than a lunchroom cafeteria / There are cliques and groups and gossip." Douglas Ray says it directly in "Chaperoning": "I want to say, 'It will get better' / in five minutes, in college, in x or y, but things might not." Such contradiction strengthens the anthology by emphasizing queerness as a site of multiple experiences and concerns.

These concerns are not always obviously related to sexuality or gender. Volpert's introduction notes that "[n]ot all the poems directly address queer matters, of course, because teachers have many things to do in a day besides pondering their own sexual orientation." Queer teachers (and students) do not stop being queer because sexuality and gender identity are not part of the lesson plan for that day. A teacher's identity does not change when, as in Miodrag Kojadinovic's "A Workday in China," he asks his students ". . . questions from the textbooks about / drugs and suicides and losing weight." Such subjects do not necessarily take on a queer flavor simply because the teacher is queer, nor do the poems contained in *This Assignment is So Gay*, as a whole, take a position as to whether they should. While Ma'ayan's poem expresses some sense of guilt at not addressing issues of sexuality, Kojadinovic's does not, even if he doubts the importance of the subjects covered in the required textbook. Such issues remain open for discussion.

How to teach, whether or not one is queer, also remains an unanswered question. The teaching methods the poems depict or imply vary. Students take tests, write essays, and keep journals. Some teachers give lectures. Ron Riekki begins "Noon in the Garden of Queer Theory and Alabama" with a brief outline of one:

> Judith Butler on the board, not allowed
> in their heads. I explain performativity,
> how they're trick-or-treating right now
> with their Dale Earnhardt Jr. ballcaps.

By contrast, the speaker of Benjamin S. Grossberg's "Secret Admirer: An Essay" says "I have learned to teach by asking questions— / because talking on with no response terrifies me" even though he himself preferred to learn from teachers who, rather than leading discussions, taught "by saying brilliant things."

Teacher-student relationships differ greatly depending on the poem as well. The speaker of Jeff Mann's "Gallery, Virginia Tech" wants to be

> . . . the ferocious
> father totemic bear
> furry and fanged
> guardian of the tribe.

He wants to protect and fight for his students. By contrast, Ralph Malachowski, in "Adjunctivitis" describes an antagonist relationship with students: "Professor, you find all my mistakes, then mark them wrong. / You're so mean." For other teachers, the roles of instructor and learner may be reversed in the way Paulo Freire advocates in *Pedagogy of the Oppressed*. In "The Introductory Poetry Class Defines Ranchera," Ruth L. Schwarz records different students' perspectives and definitions; they make meaning and knowledge together with their teacher. As their teacher makes careful notes of what the students say, instead of lecturing to note-taking students, they trade roles. Finally, the speaker of Megan Volpert's "This Is Brown Bear Soup" says she teaches like she is "on one of those cop shows where a hardcase joins the force to avenge the fact that his sister was abducted when they were kids." She will do whatever it takes—and use whatever approaches work—in the classroom. Queer teaching does not imply a single approach or pedagogical ideology any more than it suggests a simple unitary identity.

Variation in form and style occurs within a more restricted range in *This Assignment Is So Gay*. Neither traditional form nor experimentation take up much space, though Nathan Alling Long and D. Gilson contribute sonnets and Kenneth Pobo uses the spelling "str8." There are a few prose poems. Several others make use of space—with indentation, gaps in lines, and columns of text—yet most do so conservatively. What differs the most, in terms of form and style, is the level of polish. Many pieces are crafted in the way a poem in *The American Poetry Review* or in *Poetry* might be. Amanda Powell opens "Wanting the Good" with lines that express gestures of love, only to conclude with cruel words that homophobic people might use to describe them:

My hand at your neck, *perverse*
our eyes finding each other along the pillow, *unnatural*
a smile begun before we're awake, *abnormal*
our bodies milky and sallow, freckled and still, *wrong.*

The placement of these hateful words at the ends of the lines emphasizes the contrast between the meanings they carry and the love expressed in the gestures that precede them. Other poems partake in another kind of craft. There are printed versions of spoken word poems, such as Theresa Davis' "Simon Says," which concludes with capital letters simulating a shout: "Do this, and I guarantee/our young people, they will ROCK YOU!!" There are also poems that seem designed to declare that their content matters more than their form. Raye begins and ends "Big Fat Faker" with flat, straightforward language:

I'm a faker.
A big fat faker.
A liar liar pants on fire
phony
fraud
faker.

The plainness of these sentences emphasizes that what matters here is the feeling of impostor syndrome, rather than its expression. That this message is sent with form makes it paradoxical, even as it signals the importance of political and social engagement.

The diversity of *This Assignment is So Gay* leaves open the form such engagement should take. This anthology raises more questions about teaching—queer and otherwise—than it answers. Because of this openness, the anthology could be used in the classroom to spur a variety of reflective discussions about education and learning. For this same reason, it also has the potential to ignite a variety of conversations among teachers about pedagogy, identity, and courage in the classroom.

Acknowledgments

With thanks to my editor Haaris Naqvi, and the entire Bloomsbury team, for embracing this project and recognizing its audience. I couldn't hope to work with a better group of editors, designers, and marketing experts who also happen to be really nice people.

For their support and encouragement during the early stages of this project, I wish to thank friends, colleagues, and mentors Becky Bradway, Bonnie Culver, Dawn Leas, Jeanetta Calhoun Mish, and Wayne Ude.

This book is obviously a product of community support. It is precisely because of the inspiring activity in our literary communities that I felt compelled to share the endless possibilities for literary citizens both established and emerging. Thus, I offer my sincere thanks to all of my interviewees for offering their experiences and examples of what happens when we unite over shared passions.

Finally, I am ever grateful to my spouse for his endless support, coffee refills, and to-do list partnership. I may have finally found my ideal writing assistant.

Index

49 Alaska Writing Center   162
826 National   27, 110, 162

Academy of American Poets   162
Accents Publishing   89–90, 122
agents   54, 56, 65
Akashic Books   87
Ashland University   133
Association of Writers and Writing
        Programs (AWP)   39, 42,
        55, 80, 162
Astairs, Zinta   90–1
audience   x, 3, 5–6, 15–16, 20–1,
        41, 65, 102, 118, 121, 146, 153
author development   xii, 12–13,
        15, 19, 56, 59, 66, 72–3,
        85–6, 102, 114, 116, 153

Ball State University   133
Banks-Martin, Georgia Ann
        100–1, 104
Bausch, Richard   130
Beachy-Quick, Dan   76–7, 79
Beckel, Abigail   62, 64
Bell, Matt   48–9, 65, 85
Bensel, Alyse   74, 78–9

Bertram, Lillian-Yvonne   124–5,
        140–1
Bethany College   45
blogs   14, 29–30, 35, 40, 47, 50,
        63, 66, 76, 134, 157
Bloomsbury Group   1
Bockstedt, Jesse   89
Bolden, Emma   137
book clubs   42, 57
Bookcrossing.com   27
BookEnds Literary Agency   150–1
booksellers   16–18, 26, 32, 38,
        41, 51, 57, 76, 98, 124, 142
Booktrope Publishing   60–1, 97
Boss, Todd   119
Boston Book Festival   42
Boyd, Alex   69–70, 158
Bread Loaf Writers'
        Conference   124
Brevity   13
Brick Books   118
B-Trads Teaching Artist
        Alliance   5

Callaghan, Morley   147–8
camaraderie   14, 58, 126

Canadian Creative Writers and
    Writing Programs   162
Canadian Women in the Literary
    Arts (CWILA)   33, 109, 163
Carney, Jason   46
Carty, Jessie   85, 104–5
Cave Canem   33, 114–15, 124, 163
Cerand, Lauren   112
City Lit Project   163
Collagist, The   85
colonies   28, 116, 124
Colorado Review   76–7, 170
community
    author visits in   17, 31, 39,
        72, 125
    contributing to   ix, x, 8–9,
        11, 25, 35, 61, 64, 91, 140
    cross culture events   44, 116,
        118–20, 126
    engagement   5, 12, 25, 46, 54, 91
    events   x, 27, 31, 35, 118–19,
        130, 156
    fostering writers   viii, 8, 13–14,
        21, 28, 95, 112, 116,
        131–2, 159
    immersion in   viii, 8, 14, 35,
        55, 116, 131
    sustainability   xii, 4, 6, 20, 33,
        42, 64, 95–6, 101, 116
Companion Grasses   77
conferences   38–9, 69, 80, 84, 98,
        109, 124
Converse College   38
cultural engagement   57, 62
culture   x, 3, 5, 7, 10, 14, 23, 30,
        33, 37, 39–40, 44, 46, 51, 58,
        74, 80, 95, 108–9, 116, 134

Davio, Kelly   92–6, 102
Day, Cathy   23, 133
D'Erasmo, Stacey   178
Derricotte, Toi   114
Dickenson, Emily   147
Diesen, Debbie   50–1

Eady, Cornelius   114
Eastern Michigan University   2
editors   28, 54, 61–2, 68, 74, 78–9,
        85, 88, 91, 101–2, 136–7,
        150, 158
Elam, FeLicia   73
emerging writers   21, 27, 31, 34,
        45–6, 66, 95, 118, 141, 160
Emerson, Ralph Waldo   2–3, 5–6
Emerson College   39

Facebook   29, 41, 48–9, 54, 58, 71,
        117, 138–9, 150, 153
Fanelli, Brian   44, 71
Faust, Jessica   150
fellowships   28, 80, 115
Fenza, David W.   23
festivals   31, 42, 57, 81, 112, 119,
        164–5
Fitzgerald, F. Scott   147
Florio, Patricia   126
Forster, E. M.   1
Friedman, Jane   23, 95–6

Gaines-Friedler, Joy   114
Gale, Kate   6, 23, 55
Gaudry, Molly   88–9
Gauthier, Marie   58
Gay, Roxane   15, 84, 152, 158
Gemini Ink   163

Girls Write Now   27, 110–12, 163
goals   14, 69, 102, 154
Gomez, Tammy   118
GoodReads   29
greater good   xi, 8
Great Lakes Commonwealth of
    Letters   163
Green Mountains Review   116
Grub Street   163

Hemingway, Ernest   147–8
Herrick, Lee   153
Hippocampus Magazine   87, 101
Hogrefe, Rhonda   131
Hollars, B. J.   78, 176, 178
HTMLGIANT   15, 84
Hub City   38–9, 61, 98
Hudson Valley Writers'
    Center   164
Hunger Mountain   30–1,
    138–40
Hurst, Andrea   56

Idar, Nicole   141–2
InsideOut Literary Project   112
interviewing authors   29–30, 50,
    63, 72, 89, 117, 151
Iowa Writers' Workshop   133
isolation   15, 20, 84, 105, 127,
    146–8, 159

Jerome, Gillian   109
Jersey Shore Writers   126
Jones, Kaylie   87, 99, 135
Joseph, Allison   122
Joyce, James   147
Just Buffalo Literary Center   164

Kasischke, Laura   176
Kassube, Angella   119
Kaylie Jones Books   88, 97
Kenyon Review, The   68, 79–81
King, Amy   108

LaFarge, Albert   65
Lewis, Kitty McKay   118
Lewis, Monique Antonette   117
libraries   26–7, 35, 41–2, 51, 57,
    117–18, 122, 124–5, 130
Lighthouse Writers
    Workshop   164
LitBridge   152
literacy   27, 80–1, 107–8, 165
Literary Arts (Oregon)   164
literary boroughs   37, 39, 51
literary citizen   6, 23, 53, 59, 92, 96,
    105, 127, 130, 133, 145, 159
    community involvement   xii,
        18, 58, 84, 112, 115, 127, 140
    historical context   1–2, 145
literary journals   ix, 13, 15, 25–6,
    29–30, 32–3, 36, 73–4, 81,
    83, 88, 137, 141, 155
    editing   85–6, 91, 99, 158
    managing   86–7, 92–3, 95–6,
        100–1, 103–4, 158
    student-run   136–7, 141
    subscribing to   32, 95, 155
Lit Pub, The   89
Llompart, Cecilia Stormcrow   43–4
Loft Literary Center   164
Los Angeles Review   67, 74–6, 78,
    176, 178
Lucarelli, Jason   44
Lyons, Jacqueline   77, 170

McGuiggan, Jennifer   30
Maine Writers & Publishers
      Alliance   164
Making A Literary Life   28
marketing   16–18, 53, 57, 61, 65,
      80, 105
Martin, Gale   14, 49, 157
Martin, Manjula   96
Martucci, Andrea   40–2
Marvin, Cate   108
master of fine arts   38, 45, 88, 133,
      137–8, 140–1, 148
mentoring   15, 31, 87, 110–12,
      114, 117, 123, 129–30,
      139, 147
Mish, Jeanetta Calhoun   91, 153
Mockler, Kathryn   102–3
money   21, 24, 32–3, 34, 89–91,
      94–6, 100
Mongrel Empire Press   91
Montana Artists' Refuge   124
Moore, Dinty W.   7, 13, 23
Moran, Laura E. J.   5
Motionpoems   119
Muse Writers Center   164

Nash, Richard   89
National Poetry Month   118, 121
National Public Radio   120
Neighborhood Writing
      Alliance   165
New Hampshire Writers'
      Project   165
New Mirage Journal   100
New Yorker, The   7
New York State Writers
      Institute   115

Nicholson, Travis   136
Nielsen, Leslie   72, 86
Niewenhuis, Loreen   16, 25, 59,
      148, 157–8
nonprofit organizations   15, 25,
      27, 31, 33, 83, 98,
      109–11, 115
North Carolina Writers'
      Network   165
Northern Poetry Review   69, 158

Olsen, Mona Anita   89
online activity   35, 47, 49, 51, 63,
      84, 99, 122
opportunities
   creating for others   vii, xii, 20,
      23, 66, 89, 92, 117
   finding   9, 23, 65, 84
   sharing   13, 20, 27–8, 66,
      117, 122
Oputa, Ife-Chudeni   115
overextended efforts   9, 156
Owens College   131

PANK   15, 84
Paro, Maria Clara Bonetti   2
paying it forward   8, 13–14, 32,
      64, 69, 135
Pecchenino, Daniel   75–6
peers
   success of   21, 49, 146
   supporting   21, 56–7, 65, 70,
      80, 90, 131, 138, 149, 159
PEN   112, 165
   Prison Writing Program   27
Penguin   58, 64
Ploughshares   39–40, 151

Poetry Center   165
Poetry Society of America   166
Poets & Writers   161
Poets House   166
Poets' Quarterly   72, 75, 86, 180
Ponepinto, Joe   67, 74, 92–4,
        96, 102
Pound, Ezra   147
Press 53   56
Prisoner Express   166
Proctor, John   138–9
Purdue Writing Lab   78

Quiddity   20, 120–1

radio   viii, 49, 120–2
Ragdale Foundation   166
readers   15–16, 27, 29, 36, 41, 50,
        54, 60, 69, 81, 90, 124, 139
readings   5–6, 12, 19–20, 27, 36,
        117, 125, 153
    poetry   vii, x, 5, 43–4, 46
    series   6, 31, 45, 55, 58, 117,
        124, 126
Red Hen Press   6, 55
Red Room   29
Referential Magazine   85, 104
regional needs   ix, 38, 40, 91, 115,
        126, 148
rejection   15, 30, 86, 103
retreats   28
reviews   15, 29–30, 57, 63, 64, 66,
        67–81, 107, 109, 117, 134,
        139, 153, 169
    sample reviews   170, 176,
        178, 180
Rooney, Kathleen   62–4

Rose Metal Press   62–3
Rusty Toque, The   102–3

San Diego Writers, Ink   166
Savich, Zach   68, 79–81
Scratch Magazine   95
Sears, Katherine   60, 97
Seattle Arts & Letters   166
See, Caroline   23, 28, 150
Shepard, Neil   115–16
She Writes   29, 33, 123–4, 167
Siegel, Deborah   123–4
small press   63, 81, 85, 89,
        97, 123
    regional need   91, 98
    starting a small press   6, 8, 33,
        87–9, 91, 96–7
Smith, Patricia   21
Smoking Poet, The   90–1
social media   25, 29–30, 40, 48–9,
        57–8, 65, 71, 88, 134, 152
    communities   29, 35, 47, 49,
        51, 58, 123, 150, 153
solitary nature of writing   15, 20,
        84, 105, 127, 146–8, 159
Split Infinitive   141
Springer, Christina   114
Stein, Gertrude   147
StoryStudio Chicago   167
Stoykova-Klemer, Katerina
        89–90, 122
Summerlin, Nathan   47
Sundog Lit   20
Switaj, Elizabeth Kate   180

Tahoma Literary Review   92–5, 102
Talarico, Donna   87, 101, 104

Tarantini, Diane   7, 12, 125, 152
Taylor, Heather   45
Teachers & Writers
        Collaborative   135
teaching   27, 31, 46, 80, 125, 129,
        131, 133, 135–6, 138, 149
Teare, Brian   77, 170
Tekulve, Susan   37–8, 126, 136,
        149, 155, 158–9
Temple, Johnny   87
Teter, Betsy   38, 61, 98
Thibaudeau, Colleen   118
Thurber House   167
time management   21, 24–5, 33,
        37, 50, 57, 94, 101, 136, 154,
        156–8
Tupelo Press   58
Twitter   29, 49, 54, 58, 96,
        139, 152

Ude, Wayne   36, 70–1, 127, 137,
        147–8, 156–8
Umbach, Sandee Gertz   121
underserved communities   108–9,
        114–15, 124
    women   108–9, 123–4
    youth   110–11, 113, 133

van den Berg, Laura   151
Vermont College of Fine Arts   138
VIDA   33, 108, 167
Virginia G. Piper Center for
        Creative Writing   167
Volpert, Megan   180

volunteering   8, 15, 24, 30–1, 33,
        36, 83, 86, 88, 92, 94, 98, 105,
        107, 110, 113, 127, 135, 141

Warner, Jim   20–1, 120–1
Watson, Kevin Morgan   56
Whidbey Writers Workshop
        36, 137
Whitman, Walt   2–3, 6, 15, 145, 160
    Leaves of Grass   3
    Walt Whitman and The World   2
Wicoff, Kamy   111, 122–4
Windholz, Veronica   58–9, 64
Wolff, Rebecca   115
women writers   33, 108–11, 123,
        163, 167
Woolf, Virginia   1
workshops   12, 27, 35, 39, 55, 61,
        80–1, 115–16, 124, 130–2,
        137, 142–3
World Book Night   168
Writer Magazine, The   161
Writers & Books   168
Writers' Center, The   168
writers in schools   6, 27, 80, 110,
        113–14, 125, 135
writing centers   45–6
writing craft   59, 66, 72–3, 77,
        102, 153
writing life   11, 13, 27, 34, 64–5,
        73, 85, 114, 130, 140, 160

YMCA National Writer's
        Voice   168